Fear No One

N E I L V A N S E T E R S

iUniverse, Inc.
New York   Bloomington

iUniverse books may be ordered through booksellers or by contacting:

iUniverse
1663 Liberty Drive
Bloomington, IN 47403
www.iuniverse.com
1-800-Authors (1-800-288-4677)

ISBN: 978-1-4502-2091-0 (sc)
ISBN: 978-1-4502-2092-7 (hc)
ISBN: 978-1-4502-2093-4 (ebook)

Printed in the United States of America

iUniverse rev. date: 04/01/2010

Deum Timendo—Neminem Timeo

(Fearing God, I Fear No One)

Van Seters Family Crest, established 1435 AD

Contents

Preface

I have known about my grandfather's World War II experiences since I was a little boy, but the inspiration to research and write about them in more detail came only recently. The notion first came to me when I was reading the book *Man's Search for Meaning* by Viktor Frankl. In this very powerful book about his time in Auschwitz, Frankl talks about the differences between the people who survived their experiences and those who did not. He determined that the most important difference for the people who survived is that they still had something meaningful they needed to accomplish in their lives. Survivors refused to let themselves die because they felt they had to survive to complete whatever task or mission was unfinished. Frankl found that the motivation to survive because his meaning was far more powerful than that of family, money, possessions, or other supposed motivating factors. He turned this realization into a field of psychological study and treatment known as logotherapy.

While I was reading *Man's Search for Meaning,* it struck me that I didn't really understand my own grandfather's concentration camp experiences. I knew some of the stories at a surface level, and I had even read his short written history of what he had experienced. But I didn't know what the experience was like or how he had managed to survive. I really didn't even know why he had been imprisoned in the first place. I realized that I only had a simple understanding of what was a very complex experience.

I didn't decide to write this book right away. At first I thought I would just go back and re-read the original story he wrote in 1946 and then ask him a few questions about it. Given that we only had an old, faded copy that my parents had translated from Dutch and then typed on a typewriter in the early 1980s, I also decided to re-key the original book into the computer. I wanted to ensure that we would have an electronic copy that wouldn't be lost. As I typed, I found I was coming up with many questions I wanted to ask my grandfather. What was the experience like? How did the other prisoners behave? How did you respond to the guards? What survival mechanisms did you use? How did you feel during the ordeal? How did this experience affect your faith in God?

Given that my grandfather was already eighty-six years old, I thought that unless we could document the answers to some of these questions, an important part of our family history would be lost when he passed away. I decided to try to write a book that not only contained the story of what happened to him but that also contained more focus on the experience he had. I also thought it would be helpful if I could provide a little more context about the events he experienced and the locations where he was imprisoned so that future generations would get a more complete understanding of what happened.

Early in 2009, I approached my grandfather with the idea. I had already done some preliminary research and drafted an initial outline for the book. I met with him in a hotel in Vancouver in January of 2009, as he was on his way home from the trip to Mexico that is discussed in the beginning of the book. When I told him what I wanted to do, he enthusiastically agreed to the concept, and we arranged that I would interview him in regard to the details of his experience.

On February 21, I traveled to his home in Coaldale, Alberta, armed with my list of questions, the notes that I'd made, and a voice recorder to ensure I had a record of our conversations. We proceeded to talk almost non-stop for the next two days. While we talked mostly about his war-time experiences, we also talked about religion, family, and politics. I managed to record nine hours of very useful discussion for the book, and I also got the chance to get to know my grandfather in a way that I never had before.

Once I left Alberta, I continued my research into the context of the time and events described in the book, often searching through German and Dutch Web sites that were roughly translated into English by *Google Translate*. While there was plentiful information on some of the places where my grandfather was imprisoned, the information for others was a lot harder to come by. Eventually I found enough contextual information, and I was ready to start writing.

Before I started writing, I read a number of accounts by different survivors of the Nazi regime to get a sense of how others told their story. The books *Escape in to Darkness* by Sonia Games, *A Lucky Child* by Thomas Buergenthal, and *Jazz Survivor* by Ken Shuldman all served as inspiration for this book. I was also fortunate to find many more short stories and recollections from survivors on the Internet. Most of the stories are from Jewish survivors, and while my grandfather was not Jewish and did not experience the same type of systemic racism and persecution that his Jewish countrymen endured, many of the feelings and emotions he experienced in captivity are very similar.

While I could have written the whole book in Canada, without ever seeing the locations where my grandfather was imprisoned, I felt that I would be able to provide a much more complete picture of his experiences if I visited the locations myself. In the beginning of May 2009, I traveled to the Netherlands, rented a car, and proceeded to travel around to all the relevant locations. This trip was also an incredibly moving and meaningful experience, as I got a much better sense of what my grandfather's ordeals must have been like.

Even though it has been over sixty years since the events described in this book took place, once I told people what I was doing, they were all so wonderful and helpful. There was the police woman in Rotterdam who took me all around the police station looking for the war memorial. Once we found it, she also arranged for permission so that I could take photographs. As it is located within the police station, the normal approval process takes up to six weeks. Then there was the very nice man in city hall in Böhlen. When I asked if he might know where a particular monument was in the Böhlen area, he promptly took me right into his office. Not only did he ask all the other staff for help, but he also pulled up municipal maps, showed me where he thought the monument might be, and proceeded to print out copies for me. He also presented me with a beautiful book on the history of the town of Böhlen as a gift for my grandfather and me, even though I had just walked in off the street.

The trip was made even more memorable by two strange incidents that occurred while I was in Germany. I'm not sure whether these events were coincidental or whether they were God's way of sending me a message reinforcing my work on this project. Either way, they really helped me immerse myself in the stories and visualize the events as they would have happened.

The first incident occurred when I arrived in Böhlen. I had been driving across Germany for the last six hours and felt a little weary when I arrived into town. I parked my car on a side street, intending to take a little walk around the centre of town. No sooner had I gotten out of the car than an incredibly loud siren started blaring. The sound of the siren was unlike anything I had heard in North America, and it instantly reminded me of the air raid sirens I had heard in World War II movies. It had the same ascending introduction followed by a long, constant, high-pitched tone, and then the declining wind-down. Given that Böhlen was where my grandfather had experienced the heaviest Allied bombings, I could almost see the B-17s roaring past overhead.

The second incident happened a few days after the first and was even more unnerving. I was visiting the Buchenwald concentration camp in the town of Weimar. I had spent all day touring the various sections of Buchenwald and was just leaving the last area, a museum commemorating the Germans who perished at the hands of Soviet forces in the post-war era. As I was walking up the path, a little German girl with curly blond hair came running up to me, calling out, "Papi, Papi!" She had mistaken me for her father, and only when she got really close up did she realize her mistake. My knees almost buckled. Not only had this never happened to me before, but this was almost the exact event that had happened to my grandfather sixty-five years before when he first knocked on the door of Elizabeth Slösser's home. As described in chapter 6, her young, curly-haired, blond daughter had mistaken him for her father and had called out the same exact words. To make things even more disturbing, I was within fifty kilometres of the place where Elizabeth had lived. Before I could really compose myself, the girl was gone, leaving me with a memory that I will never forget.

The trip brought to life what my grandfather had been telling me. I could see the places he had stayed and could talk to people who really understood the history of what had occurred. I could see the camps he described and get a better sense of what it would mean to be imprisoned there. I could also get a feeling of the surrounding areas that he had been through, and the distances he had traveled. And finally, I could bring back pictures and stories of some of the places he himself had not seen for many years.

While the main purpose of my trip was to see and photograph some of the important locations described in the book, I purposely ensured that I had more time than I needed to simply visit the sites. As such, I was able to use the extra time I had to work on writing the book while the experiences were still fresh in my mind.

I wrote most of the section about my grandfather's time in the German labour camps while I was staying in the only hotel in the town of Böhlen. I could look out of my hotel window and see the power plant that stands near the site where he was imprisoned. I could also tour around the old coal mine sites, imagining what it must have been like to hide in the mine shafts as bombs fell all around.

I wrote all the sections regarding my grandfather's imprisonment in the Netherlands. I was staying at my parents' cottage in the small village of Erm, located in the province of Drente. While I was writing, I was within a few hours' drive of all the different locations where my grandfather had been imprisoned in the Netherlands.

In the same spirit, once I had completed the first draft of the book, I gave it to my brother, Nathan, and he edited it while on vacation in the Netherlands. Similarly, my mother, Janey, took her editorial turn on the second draft while also staying in Erm.

Given that the target audience for this book will not have an extensive knowledge of the events during and preceding World War II, I have tried to add some detail to give the context of my grandfather's experiences. Specifically, I have tried to include details about the different locations where he was held, why he ended up where he did, and how those locations were relevant to the larger war story. I have also added maps and pictures of all the key locations, so that people reading this book will get a better picture of where the events described in this book took place.

This book is not meant to be a complete history book of what happened in the Netherlands and Germany in 1944 and 1945. The information I have chosen is mostly focused on providing context to my grandfather's experiences, not explaining everything that was happening at the time (that would take a thousand-plus page book like *Rise and Fall of the Third Reich*). Even so, I hope that this work inspires the next generation to learn more about such an important time in our family, country, and world history.

Note from Jake Van Seters

I want to acknowledge with deep gratitude a number of dearly loved people.

First, the author of this book: Neil Van Seters. Thank you, Neil, for turning out what started as an interest and evolved into a dream, eventually culminating with the completion of this wonderful book. Thank you also for the countless hours, extensive research, and considerable traveling you invested before you even put pen to paper. I want you to know that I will never forget the many wonderful and sometimes difficult hours we spent together discussing and contemplating the events that are included in this publication. Most of all, I am deeply grateful that you respected my wishes in the focus and vision of this book. It is my prayer that *Fear No One* will be received in the spirit it was written.

I also want to express my gratitude to Tante Mar, the late wife of my brother Neil. It was her initial vision that the letter I had written shortly after my experience in the concentration camps be saved for posterity. She immediately saw the value of the document and asked that she be allowed to copy it for others to benefit from.

In the same vein, my son, Peter Van Seters, and his wife, Janey, recognized the importance the original document could have for future generations and spent many hours translating the letter from the original Dutch to English.

There were many others who provided an invaluable service, from editing to giving advice to lending a listening ear. You know who you are. Thank you from my heart!

And, most of all, I give thanks to my heavenly Father. The Van Seters' family crest has the motto *Deum Timendo—Nemien Timeo* (Fearing God, I Fear No One). It is ultimately this fear in my God and Father, along with the knowledge of the redeeming work of his Son, Jesus Christ, and the comfort of the Holy Spirit that has sustained me during my life.

In conclusion, I would like to share with you one of my favourite Psalms. The Psalms of David were especially important to me during my captivity.

They were the part of God's Living Word that I turned to time and again for strength and comfort. The following is taken from Psalm 66. I take the words as they are put to music in the Book of Praise (Anglo-Genevan Psalter).[i]

> Come and be to my words attentive,
>
> All you who the Almighty fear.
>
> Let me declare how He has helped me,
>
> How in my troubles He drew near.
>
> I cried to God in my affliction,
>
> And He in mercy heard my voice;
>
> I sang His praise with exultation.
>
> In His compassion I rejoice.

—Jake Van Seters, 2009

Chapter 1: Introduction

At first glance, there was nothing too unusual about that particular Wednesday in Puerto Vallarta, Mexico. It was November 26, 2008, and like most warm days, the beach was packed with sun-worshipping tourists getting too much sun. As is common in a Mexican tourist town, visitors were enjoying the choice of a number of water sports in the warm tropical ocean. Among the beach crowd that day were jet skiers, power boaters, wind surfers, and scuba divers. If you had looked up in the sky, you would have seen someone parasailing, their feet dangling some one hundred feet in the air behind the power boat to which they were attached. After about twenty minutes spent enjoying the aerial view of the town, the crew decided it was time for the ride to end. They set out a target on the beach, and the thrill-seeking passenger glided in for a perfect landing. Nothing in this story is out of the ordinary, as such a scene plays out repeatedly most days on this particular beach—nothing, that is, except that the parasailer is Jacob Van Seters Sr., that he is my grandfather, and that he is eighty-six years old.

Meet Jake

It's admittedly a little strange for an eighty-six-year-old man to go parasailing. Most men of that age struggle to stay mobile, let alone take part in high-adrenaline sports. If this incident had been unique, you might think that Jake had a momentary lapse of reason. But this type of activity isn't out of the ordinary for my grandfather. He's a man who bought a thirty-five-foot boat he named the *Double Dutch* and learned to sail when he was sixty-seven. He designed and helped build his own cabin a few years later. He built a workshop behind his cabin and stocked it with woodworking tools when he was eighty-four. To this day, he uses that shop to make wooden furniture that he designs himself.

There are more examples of what sets Jake apart, but suffice it to say that he is not like most men his age. For that matter, he's not like most men of any age. With his passion for life and his refusal to let the fact that he's getting older stop him from doing the things he loves, he's an inspiration to many of those who know and love him.

Jake didn't become who he is today because his life was easy and carefree. He has had to deal with issues and circumstances far more difficult than what most people will ever experience. While there are many factors that collectively shaped the way Jake is today, none were so powerful or so life altering as his experiences during World War II. Like so many other Dutchmen, Jake was abducted by the Germans, sent to Germany, and forced to work for almost a year under inhuman conditions to help fuel the German war machine.

The Source Material

There are two main resources that provide the base material for retelling Jake's experiences during this time. First, we are fortunate to have a copy of the thirty-page account that he wrote about his experiences shortly after the war ended. Written in 1946, this letter documented many of the events that happened during his time in Germany. Second, Jake and I met for two days to discuss his experiences during the war. I recorded these discussions and produced a written transcript of the nine hours of dialogue.

The combination of the 1946 written account and the 2009 interviews provides a very interesting and complimentary foundation for this book. Given that the first account was written so soon after the war, many of the details are very accurate. This includes the dates when certain events occurred, the people involved, and some of the finer details around how the events unfolded. However, at that time Jake had not yet had the time to really deal with some of the emotional aspects of his ordeal, so his retelling of his experiences as a prisoner is very matter of fact. In addition, there are at least a few stories that he didn't feel comfortable sharing at that time. By the time we had our discussions sixty-three years later, some of the factual elements may have faded a little in Jake's mind (although most of the details are as sharp as ever). On the other hand, given that he has had many years to think and reflect on what happened, he was in a much better position to relate the real experience he went through: what he saw, how it felt, and how others behaved. He was also much more emotionally prepared to discuss the experience he had rather than just relating the factual story of what happened. Combined, the source documents paint a much richer picture of what actually happened than either would on its own.

The contextual information for this book came from many different sources. The information from the Netherlands portions of the story came from books and documentaries on the Dutch experience during the war, from information gathered from the actual sites where Jake was held captive, and from various historical accounts from other survivors. The information for the German labour camps was a little harder to find. Both locations where Jake was a prisoner were fairly small and located in former East Germany. As such, English language information about these sites was fairly difficult to come by. But gradually, with enough translated searches through Dutch and German Web sites, I was able to piece together a relatively accurate picture of these locations as well.

What Really Matters

The title of this book, *Fear No One,* was not chosen at random. These words are taken from the Latin motto that graces the Van Seters' family crest, a copy of which is located in the middle pictorial section of this book. This crest was first developed in 1435 and has been an important family symbol ever since. The complete Latin phrase from the crest reads, *Deum Timendo—Neminem Timeo* or *Fearing God, I Fear No One.* In this context, the first use of the word "fear" has a different meaning than the second; they are purposely combined to highlight the contrast between the two meanings. To "fear God" means to have a reverent faith that the world is in God's hand and under his control. The second use of the word "fear" is the more common use associated with being afraid. So in other words, the phrase could read, "Because I have faith that God is in control of all things, I have no reason to be afraid of anyone."

This powerful phrase is very important to our family. It expresses the conviction that, as a family, we draw our strength from a living God who can protect and take care of us; therefore, there is no one on this earth that we need to fear. Jake knew this phrase very well and thought of it often during his ordeal. It gave him the strength he needed to carry on, even when things looked very bleak.

As you will see in this book, Jake experienced many emotions during his year of captivity. There was sorrow, anger, despair, disgust, and even some defiance. But he was almost never afraid. It was this lack of fear that Jake believes helped keep him alive. Prisoners who were afraid simply didn't last. Jake explains the danger of fear in the following way:

> The worst thing you could have was fear. Fear stinks. Take animals. I had chickens, and if there was a weak one, they would go after it, pecking it and pulling its feathers out. Then they get the raw skin, they get blood, and then they kill it. They all go for the scared one. The same happens with people. I had it several times with people at the camp. I was with a guy named Heiser. I said, "Look straight," because if you look scared they see it right way; they smell it. The way he acted you could see he was scared. "Why is he scared?" the Germans thought. "He must have done something wrong." It makes them suspicious. Once you are afraid, there is no cure and you cannot stop it.

The photo on the cover of this book expresses similar sentiments. The image is of *The Stone Man*, a statue commemorating the struggle of concentration camp prisoners. The statue sits in the shooting range at Kamp Amersfoort, one of the camps where Jake was imprisoned by the Germans. *The Stone Man* represents all the malnourished, abused prisoners who were imprisoned there during the war. There are three elements to this statue that are very important. The left hand is open as an expression of the despair prisoners felt over their circumstances, as well as what was happening to their families while they were locked up. The clenched right hand represents the unbroken willpower that the prisoners needed to survive. And most importantly, the gaze of the statue is to the heavens, symbolizing that, to survive, the prisoners needed to look beyond what was happening at the camp and draw their strength from God.

While the stories of what happened to Jake for the year he was imprisoned are both amazing and inspiring, he would be the first to say that his survival is not of his own doing. By himself he would have never made it. It was only through the grace and providence of God that he could endure and survive. As you will see throughout his story, God was always there with him, keeping him safe and ensuring that he never suffered more than he could bear. And that should be the most inspiring element of all.

Chapter 2: Life in Prewar Netherlands

To appreciate what life was like in the Netherlands prior to World War II, it is necessary to take a brief look back at the prior decades. The Netherlands had remained neutral during World War I, following a tradition of neutrality that dated back to 1815. While the countries around them slaughtered each other in World War I, the Dutch managed to stay on the sidelines. Given that the Dutch were a nation of traders, they were still greatly affected by the naval blockages that cut off their shipping lanes. However, while their economy suffered and unemployment was rampant, they were spared the death and destruction experienced by many of the countries around them.

As World War I ended, the Netherlands was left in a fairly advantageous position. It was not saddled with war debt or a need to rebuild infrastructure. As a result, the Dutch economy thrived after the war. Prosperity continued for years, right up to the time of the great depression of the 1930s. The slowdown of the depression era hit the Dutch as hard, if not harder, than the other countries of Europe. The Dutch government was far more conservative than some of their peers and did not invest in relief projects the way the Americans had. By the late 1930s, the Netherlands was in a difficult economic position, with high unemployment and considerable unrest among the population.

Across the border, things in Germany were markedly different. As Hitler took control, the economy began to grow. It continued to thrive into the late 1930s, and many Dutchmen were lured across the border in search of work. While there was concern within the Netherlands at the growing military might of their German neighbours, most felt that Dutch neutrality would be respected in the way it had been in the past. Some Dutch people favoured a formal alliance with the English and the French, but most were skeptical due to the inaction of those countries when Czechoslovakia was invaded by the Germans. The decision was made to declare neutrality and trust that Germany would honour the declaration as they had in World War I. Nevertheless, the mood in the Netherlands as the war approached was one of general unrest and uneasiness among the population.[ii]

Life on the Islands

Jake's early years in the south of the Netherlands set the stage for what he went through during the war and how he would manage to cope and survive. Jake was just eleven years old when Hitler took power in Germany in 1933. He and his family lived in the small town of Dirksland on the then-isolated island of Goeree-Overflakkee, south of the city of Rotterdam. At that time there were no bridges to the island, so all traffic came and went by boat. The community was largely supported by farming, and Dirksland contained a number of small businesses that supported the local farming industry.

The area was just entering the modern era. Some people owned cars, but many still relied on a horse and a cart to move things around. Trucks and tractors were available, but they were typically a privilege reserved for the few lucky enough to be able to afford them. As a result of the town's isolation, the events of the outside world, while interesting, had little immediate impact on this small rural community.

The Van Seters were one of two milling families in town, taking the wheat the farmers grew and turning it into flour for the bakers to use in their bread. They had a mill located on one of the dykes that ran along the canals, just up from the centre of town. Originally this had been a classic Dutch windmill, but most of it had been demolished and rebuilt in a more modern fashion. By the time the war began, the mill was a low-rise building that operated from power supplied by a diesel motor, instead of traditional wind power. Given the role they played in the farming economy, the Van Seters family was an important cog in the operations of the small town of Dirksland.

The young people on the islands grew up in a very isolated fashion compared to those who lived in the more metropolitan centres of Rotterdam, Amsterdam, and the Hague. They had limited ability to connect with what was happening in the rest of the world. As Jake often accompanied his father to Rotterdam, he did have a little more exposure to the outside world than most of the other young people. That said, like most other islanders, he was still very ill prepared for the realities of the coming war.

As a result of their isolation, the culture of the islands was very conservative. Young people did not have much freedom to make their own decisions; everything was decided for them by their parents. For instance, when Jake was seventeen, he desperately wanted to go to the architectural school in Delft. He had done very well in trade school, and the director of the school went to his mother to suggest that Jake should pursue his studies further. But his mother would have none of it, insisting that he had to work in the mill. The issue was never raised again.

This is not to imply that growing up on the islands was not an enjoyable experience. While there was work to be done, there was also time for leisure. Jake was very active and involved in several sports. He also had a girlfriend, Iet, who he loved very much and whom he could see on a fairly regular basis.

When he was younger, he had the opportunity to participate in the local boy scouts organization, only one of about forty boys on the island who got to do so. The boy scouts was a much more serious organization in those times, and Jake earned merit badges for learning a variety of camping and survival skills. On one occasion, he even got to represent the local scout troop and shake the hand of the Queen when she came to the island.

The Boy Miller

A significant year for the Van Seters family was 1933. Jake's father, Arie Van Seters, died that year, leaving Jake as the head of the family. On his deathbed, Arie made Jake promise that he would look after the family. He told Jake that God would help him but that he had to be the instrument. Jake promised his father that he would do everything in his power to take care of the family. Even at a young age, Jake believed that your word is your bond. He was determined to do whatever it took to fulfill his promise.

While such a request may have been too much to ask of an eleven-year-old, his father really had no other choice. In the 1930s, the Netherlands did not have the same social and economic safety nets that exist in many first-world countries today. There was no unemployment insurance program, and there were definitely no welfare handouts. The only real source of support at the time came from the church deaconry, but their funds were very limited. The congregations that supported them had very little money to donate due to the hard economic times, and therefore the churches had very little to disperse. It wasn't that people didn't want to give; they just didn't have the ability. Just about the only people with any real money at that time were the big farm owners. Unfortunately, they were far less generous than they should have been, considering the need that existed.

While it may sound terrible to modern ears, in those days the poor and widowed would often become destitute and even die of hunger. At the very least, they would be abused and taken advantage of by local businessmen. So, while Jake's mother may have taken advantage of Jake's promise and his loyalty at the time, she also had little other choice.

Jake faced several challenges as he assumed a leadership position in the family. First and foremost was the fact that his father had been terrible at managing money and had left a large amount of debt for the next generation. The situation was so bad that when his father died, he had accumulated debts amounting to twice the value of the mill. The second big challenge concerned the mill manager who was now running the mill. As Jake was still young, he found himself reporting to this manager. The problem was that the mill was still losing money and was getting further into debt. Given what he understood of the business, this didn't make much sense to Jake. He became convinced that the manager was skimming funds from the operation and was therefore the cause of the continual losses they were incurring. His mother, the trusting soul that she was, didn't believe him until he could produce absolute proof of what was going on. Only when it became blatantly obvious that the manager was stealing was he finally fired. Jake had to take over running the mill at the tender age of sixteen.

The challenges that Jake faced in the mill only grew once he took full control. The mill was buried in debt, and the creditors were demanding payment. Now that he was in control of the finances, Jake would make every effort to pay those creditors, even if it meant less money to go around at home. As a result, he often frustrated his mother, who wanted more money to run the household. To Jake it really wasn't their money; it was the creditors' money, and his first priority was ensuring they were repaid.

Although Jake had the best intentions in terms of repaying what he owed, the challenge he faced was enormous. There was a mortgage on the property of twenty thousand guilders, or roughly the equivalent of the cost of seven new, free-standing houses. That was in addition to other secondary loans that his father had obtained. Jake had no help and no one to go to for assistance or advice, so the pressure really took its toll. Fortunately, the holder of the mortgage lowered the amount owed to ten thousand guilders, as it would have been no use to him if the mill had gone bankrupt.

Once the manager was gone, the mill started turning a profit again. As he had no arrangements in writing, Jake became increasingly worried that the mortgage holder would increase the mortgage back to twenty thousand guilders and that he would charge for the unpaid interest. The idea of all that debt made him panic a little. He thought, "Why should I work the rest of my life just to get out of a hole that I didn't make?"

When he was seventeen years old, Jake went to the mortgage holder and told him that unless he put in writing that the mortgage was going to be ten thousand guilders, he could have the mill. With the way business licenses worked at that time, Jake would have been able to take his equipment and operate out of a rented facility, while the mortgage holder would not have been able to operate as a miller. Jake reassured the man that he had full right to the total sum, and that he would not be angry if he insisted on payment. He did promise, however, that if the mortgage was lowered, he would pay it off without anymore issues. It was a big step for the mortgage holder, but he did agree to the lower amount.

At the same time that Jake renegotiated his mortgage, the economy started to improve. Because the army was being mobilized, the ranks of the unemployed shrank by five hundred thousand. People were being paid decent wages again. Through a lot of hard work, Jake paid back the entire debt by the time he was twenty-three. His timing on the negotiation had been very fortuitous. If he had tried to get the same break a few months later, the mortgage holder would never have agreed.

A Unique Combination of Experience

By the time the Germans invaded the Netherlands, Jake's combination of life experiences had left him better prepared to deal with the war than many around him. He had grown up quickly due to the premature death of his father and the additional responsibilities he had taken on. He was therefore much more mature and seasoned than many others his age. He was also very physically fit, due to a combination of the manual nature of his work, as well as the sports in which he participated. He had good mechanical skills from having to keep the mill running on his own. He had a mother who depended on him, and he had to act as a father figure for his youngest brother. Plus, he had learned basic survival skills, so he knew how to take care of himself in the woods and how to avoid detection.

It was as if the experiences of his youth had been carefully orchestrated to prepare him for the events that were to come. Looking back, it is very clear to Jake that the hand of the Lord was guiding his development even then. Today he is not sure that he would have survived the war without the unique set of circumstances that prepared him for his ordeal.

Chapter 3: Living with German Occupation

In late 1939 and early 1940, there were those in the Netherlands who thought that Dutch neutrality would still be respected. What they did not know was that Germany had never intended to respect Dutch neutrality and had always planned to invade. In fact, the Germans had plans of turning the Netherlands into a German state and incorporating the Dutch into the German population. The Nazi party viewed the Dutch as part of the Aryan race, and they saw them as having particularly strong genetics. In a sense, they thought that by incorporating the Dutch people into their own society, they would strengthen their own gene pool.

Many Dutch people also clung to the notion that if Germany did invade, Britain would come to their rescue with their mighty navy. Unfortunately, most people in the Netherlands had little insight into the real power of Germany and the unfortunate weakness of the British. Since people in the Netherlands would tune into the BBC from London, they were constantly exposed to propaganda relating to the strength of the British forces and how they could counter the Nazi threat. They also had no clue how powerful their German neighbours had become in the last decade. They would soon understand just how badly they had misjudged the situation.[iii]

The Invasion

Any thoughts of the British coming to the rescue began to fade when they failed to respond once Denmark and Norway fell to the Germans in April of 1940. So the Netherlands stepped up their efforts to counter a possible invasion. On May 10, the German army violated Dutch neutrality by crossing the border and storming into the Netherlands. At first the Germans urged the Dutch to offer no resistance and place themselves under their "protection," whereby the

Germans would guarantee Dutch independence and allow the monarchy to stay in place.

When the Dutch government refused to give in, they were quickly exposed to the real power of the Nazi juggernaut. On the first day of the invasion, the German troops destroyed almost the whole Dutch air force, including all of their modern planes. All the Dutch had left on day two of the invasion were some old World War I era bi-planes. The Germans dropped paratroopers into the Hague to try to capture the Queen, but she had been spirited off to London aboard a British destroyer.

Even though the Germans were rapidly over-running the Netherlands, the fact that they had to spend five days fighting Dutch resistance was causing them to get a little impatient. They had intended the whole operation to be over in one day, so even though the outcome was assured, the delay was starting to frustrate the German command. They gave the Dutch an ultimatum: give up or we'll start leveling Dutch cities with our bombers. This threat was enough to convince the Dutch, and they began the process of negotiating their surrender.

Unfortunately, due to lack of communications, the order to bomb the city of Rotterdam was given anyway, and the city centre was leveled by German bombers. Nine hundred people died, and seventy-eight thousand were left homeless. Any remaining overt Dutch resistance vanished, and the Netherlands was established as a Nazi state. The only part of the Dutch army that had offered real resistance was the Marines, as they were well trained and well equipped. But even they were forced to give up rather than see their country destroyed.[iv]

A Short History of the Occupied Netherlands

Once the Germans had full control, they appointed a new civilian governor to rule the Netherlands. This was a different system than that of countries like France and Norway, who had separate puppet governments established. As Germany intended to integrate the Netherlands into the German homeland, they felt that extending the German government system into the Netherlands was the most appropriate arrangement. The man they chose for the job was an Austrian Nazi, Arthur Seyss-Inquart, who supported the idea of the Netherlands becoming a German province.

One of the first things that the Nazis did when they took over the Netherlands was to pass a law that banned any communist or socialist parties.

This was expanded a year later to include all parties other than the Nazi party. This second step severely curtailed the influences of the religious groups in the Netherlands, as the political movements they had established were now outlawed. The Nazis replaced the existing Dutch system of justice with their own and placed all labour unions under the direct control of the government. The press was also affected, as newspapers were highly censored and all radio stations were placed under Nazi control.

The Nazis started deporting Jews from the Netherlands shortly after they arrived. When the first group was shipped out of the country, the Dutch people held a national strike to protest. On February 25, 1941, people across the country stopped working, with more than 50 percent of the municipal workers in Amsterdam going on strike. It had little effect on slowing the Nazis down, and going on strike only served to infuriate them. The strike was quickly broken, and its leaders were executed. The Nazis fired the mayor of Amsterdam for not being tough enough on the strikers and fined the city 15 million guilders.

The deportation of Dutch Jews continued in earnest. The Nazis were particularly successful in their pursuit of the Jews in the Netherlands, deporting a higher percentage than any other occupied country outside of Poland. They set up an elaborate network of transit camps to ensure that the Jews were efficiently removed from the country. Of the one hundred forty thousand Jews that had lived in the Netherlands before the war began, only thirty thousand remained by 1945.

There are several explanations for the high death rate among the Dutch Jews. First, the Dutch state kept excellent records of its people, and therefore, it was very easy to find out who was Jewish and who was not. Second, most Dutch Jews simply did not believe that they would be the subject of genocide. Most believed the Nazi propaganda regarding why they were being rounded up. In his book *163256: A Memoir of Resistance*, Michael Englishman talks about how even the Dutch Jewish Congress downplayed the Nazi threat through a policy of *shaa still* (keep quiet). The congress was concerned that spreading the reports of what was happening to Jews in other countries would cause undue alarm in the Jewish community.[v] Third, the non-Jewish Dutch people really couldn't believe that the Jews were going to be sent to death camps. Finally, it was punishable by death to help Jews or hide them in your home. Over a third of the people who chose to ignore the risk and help the Jews anyway ended up perishing during the war.

An active resistance to the German occupation arose in the Netherlands in the form of the Dutch Underground. The landscape in the Netherlands made their task quite difficult, though; it's very difficult to hide when you operate in a flat, open country with no mountains and few forests. They did find ways to produce forged ration cards and counterfeit money, distribute underground newsletters, collect intelligence, and sabotage key facilities (phone lines, roads, railways, etc). As the war progressed, they began coordinating the hiding of Jews, drafted Dutch loyalists on the run, downed allied air force pilots, and others who were being pursued by the Germans. Involvement in the Underground came at a heavy price, for if they were caught, people could expect to be sentenced to death.

There was also a group of Dutch people who helped the incoming German invaders. The National Socialist Movement (NSB) was the only legal political party in the Netherlands during the war, and they actively colluded with the Germans. The leader of this party was a man named Anton Mussert, who desperately wanted to become leader of the county.

The NSB party membership grew to about one hundred thousand during the war, and most local government officials were selected from the ranks of the NSB. Members of the NSB called on the rest of the Netherlands to reject the old Dutch government that had fled to England and to embrace the new regime. They also played a large role in helping the Nazis round up as many Dutch Jews as possible. That said, the Nazis never seriously considered making Anton Mussert the leader of the country, as they thought him to be a bit of a fool. Once the Netherlands were liberated, Anton Mussert was tried as a traitor and sentenced to death.

By 1944, the tide of the war had really started to shift toward the Allied forces. When their troops invaded France at Normandy in June of 1944, the Dutch people thought they would soon be liberated. The Allied forces captured the city of Maastricht on September 13 and shortly thereafter liberated other small southern parts of the country through an attack known as Operation Marketgarden. Unfortunately, this offensive fell well short its goals, and most of the provinces in the Netherlands had to wait until 1945 to be liberated.

The situation in the Netherlands in the winter of 1944 was made much worse by very cold weather and a severe lack of food throughout the country. There was no coal or wood available for heating, and no running water or working sewage systems. Food supplies from outside the cities had virtually stopped, and any available food had to be severely rationed. People in Amsterdam were surviving on 450 calories per day, and some resorted to eating tulip bulbs just to stay alive. Sixteen thousand people died that winter while waiting for liberation.

On May 5, 1945, the Germans finally gave up control of the Netherlands through a negotiated surrender, and the last of the western provinces were freed. The war had cost the Netherlands 205,900 lives or 2.36 percent of their population, the highest death rate any of the occupied countries in Western Europe.[vi]

Understanding the German System

If one were to ask Jake how he was able to survive and at times even thrive under German occupation and imprisonment, he will say that one of the key reasons was that he really understood the Germans. He understood the way they were brought up, the way they thought, and how their whole societal structure worked. Once they came to the island, Jake made a point of learning everything about them. He was a keen observer of their patterns of behavior, always trying to figure what he could get away with and how he could avoid getting caught.

Jake has often said that he would have never made it if he had been in a Japanese camp. He feels that his lack of understanding of their system and culture would have meant he wouldn't have been able to cope with what was going on. While he was under German rule, he saw many horrific things, but at least he understood why they were happening, as well as the rationale of the individuals carrying out the actions.

During the times he was locked up, Jake knew how to deal with the guards and the SS. He would always try to refer to a person with a higher rank than they actually had; a huge compliment in a hierarchical culture. He ensured that he never belittled his captors, as that pretty much guaranteed abusive treatment. He also always figured how much authority a particular person had so he would know the areas where he could push and where he would likely get into trouble. Finally Jake understood that in a very hierarchical system, there always had to be an answer (even if it was not the truth) and the paperwork always had to be in order. He exploited that fact to his advantage several times during his captivity.

There is a saying in German, *Befehl ist Befehl*, meaning *Orders are Orders*. While it may seem trite to us today, the whole German culture of the time was built around this principle. Children were taught this from a very young age, and it was reinforced in schools and the workplace. The Nazis built on this cultural foundation but took it to an entirely new level.

The totalitarian system of command and control essentially meant that you either followed orders or you were shot. There was no room for questioning or discussion. And because the German people had grown up in a culture that supported doing what you were told, they accepted and even embraced the Nazi party. In her book *My Father's Country*, Wibke Bruhns documents her father's role in Nazi Germany and shows how he, among others, never questioned what was happening. Even in his private correspondence, he seemed to support every move the government made.[vii]

The effects of the "orders are orders" culture accounted both for the success and the failure of the Nazi party. The German troops always fought fiercely because they knew the consequences of retreating. In the initial stages of the war, the Germans were able to roll over the weaker countries around them. The German army became very efficient in doing exactly what they were told. The real problems arose when the things they were told to do were not so wise. Whether it was during the failed Battle of Britain or the even more disastrous invasion of Russia, the German system did not have the flexibility to allow the troops to adapt to the changing conditions around them. When the enemy started reacting in ways that the German high command did not anticipate or comprehend, their troops on the ground remained invested in destructive strategies.

The Edges of the Underground

Jake and his brothers, Neil and Hugo, could see the bombing of Rotterdam from their island home. No one was quite sure what was happening, but there was mass confusion and hysteria. Rumors were flying around town, with most being quite exaggerated. The fight also came to the island, as the remaining planes of the Dutch military tried to put up a fight against the German *Luftwaffe* (the German air force). Unfortunately, the Dutch were hopelessly outclassed and were getting shot out of the sky at an alarming rate.

One of the Dutch planes was shot down near Dirksland. Seeing the plane go down, Jake and his brothers went on their bikes to investigate. They found that the pilot had parachuted out of the plane and was sitting on the side of the road smoking a cigarette. While he was obviously very nervous, he was also quite brave. He told the boys he was going to find someone to drive him back to the airport so he could go back and fight some more. While they were still talking, the German pilot who had shot down the Dutch plane came back around and started strafing them with bullets in an attempt to finish the job.

They all had to dive in to a ditch to avoid getting shot. They still had a lot to learn about the realities of war.

The fact that the three of them were out in the open, talking to a pilot who had just been shot down, illustrated how little the people of the island understood about modern war. Dutch farmers would still ride out on motorcycles, armed with pitchforks, thinking they were going to fight downed German air force pilots. They had not been exposed to modern warfare. The country was equipped with old guns, old tanks, and old planes. The only parts of their army that was somewhat respectable were the navy and the marines. The average Dutch citizen could not even imagine the firepower that the German army possessed.

Once the fighting was over, things settled back into a normal routine quite quickly. While the Germans took over the operations of the country, they left a lot of the administrative infrastructure in place. They even let most of the Dutch army return home, as they saw the troops as too ill-trained and ill-equipped to be of much use to their war efforts.

For the first few years of the occupation, the Germans behaved quite civilly to most of the population. While they were starting to round up the Jews, they didn't rape, kill, or pillage the local inhabitants. Jake even remembers that a certain German soldier was accused of rape and was executed in a public square for his crime. As a result, there was a portion of Dutch society that began to sympathize with the Germans and would help them in any way they could.

Though the Germans were not overtly cruel in the beginning, their mere presence infuriated most of the Dutch population. It was no different on the island. Jake and his friends were determined to do whatever they could to make the Germans miserable. They would move road signs, put sugar in the gas tanks of German officers, and paint pro-Dutch and anti-German slogans on roadways. One time they directed a whole column of German tanks down a small one-way road. As the road eventually came to a dead end, the Germans had a tough time getting everything turned around. While these were not major acts of sedition, they were indicative of the hostile feelings that existed toward the Germans.

Unfortunately, the time of German restraint was not to last. As they did not receive the cooperation they wanted from the island population, they increased their level of aggression. The Nazi soldiers became more and more brutal. They would push people into the harbor if they got annoyed and would then let them drown. If the locals participated in an act of rebellion, the Germans would take five men from the town and shoot them in the public square as an act of retaliation. They also implemented a strict rationing system, where everyone got a pre-set amount of coupons for food. The Germans even considered the trading of these coupons as black-market activity and would send anyone they caught engaged in this activity to the concentration camps.

It was during this time of increasing German control that Jake and Neil constructed a hiding place within his mill. They were intent on keeping people from either being executed or sent to the camps.

In those days, there was no public water system, so most places had some sort of rain capture system to ensure they had reliable access to drinking water. In the mill, there was a rain pipe that came down from the roof and went into a large tank under the machine room. The machine room was about three metres wide by five metres long and housed a very large forty-horsepower engine and three thousand-pound flywheel. The engine took up much of the space, so to get to the reservoir there was only a small access plate in the floor on one side of the room.

The brothers emptied the reservoir and constructed a wall that split the now-empty room in two. They put some simple furnishings in the room on the far side and installed a light. They then refilled the portion closer to the access plate with water. That way, if anyone opened the panel, all they would see was the water that belonged in the reservoir.

During the war, the Van Seters family hid many British air force pilots and convicted Dutchmen in that secret room. If they were caught they would have received an automatic death penalty, but given the cleverness of the design, the secret room was never discovered.

The challenge in hiding people was in feeding them, for these individuals did not have ration cards. If Jake's family used the normal channels to get food, they would not have had enough to go around. Fortunately, as they had a mill, they could trade excess flour and feed with other people. They would get piglets from farmers who would then under-report the number of actual births. They would raise the pigs and slaughter them for meat. Jake also managed to get a cow and kept it in a three metre by five metre room in the house. Fortunately for Jake and his family, their neighbours legally kept cows, so that if their own cow made any noise, outsiders would assume it came from next door and would not report them to the Nazis.

The whole family had a role to play in helping out. While Jake's mother cooked extra food, Jake and Neil handled all the logistics of getting people in and out. Even Hugo helped out by acting as a messenger for the people in hiding. As he was just a boy, no one suspected him of anything. There were times when there were Germans staying in the house and Hugo would get messages to the people in hiding anyway. He just stood by a pipe that led into the chamber and would start relieving himself against the outside wall. As this was normal practice at the time, no one thought twice about it, even though he was really passing messages back and forth.

This was also the time when the Germans started getting a lot more aggressive toward the Jews. Jake and some of his friends tried to convince the local Jews that they were in a lot of danger and offered to help them into hiding. But like those in many other parts of the Netherlands, the Jews on the island obeyed the German orders to go to the designated gathering places and wear the Star of David. Since the Germans made no mention of concentration camps, many of the local Jews thought they would be fine. As much as Jake and the others tried to convince them that if they went they would likely not come back, most went to the meeting places. The Jews did ask Jake and his friends to hide their belongings for them until they returned. While this was also an offense punishable by death, Jake and his friends did so willingly. Unfortunately, most of the Jews were sent to Westerbork in the northeastern corner of the Netherlands. From there, the majority were sent on to either the Auschwitz extermination camp (fifty-six thousand) or the Sobibor extermination camp (thirty-five thousand). Of those sent to Sobibor, only nineteen survived.

Years later when the Jews didn't return, Jake looked through the possessions they had left and found that they had split what they could between multiple locations. As an example, they would store all their left shoes with one family and their right shoes with another, to help ensure that they could not be used or sold. Even though Jake and his friends were risking their lives to help them, the local Jews didn't trust them not to steal from their possessions. While that lack of trust saddened Jake, given what the Jewish community in the Netherlands endured, it was hardly surprising. In total, one hundred and ten thousand Jews were deported from the Netherlands and only five thousand returned alive. Over 75 percent of the Jewish population was exterminated.

The brothers were also part of the Dutch Underground movement that fed information back to the allies about what the Germans were up to. While they had no clue as to how the whole system worked, they had a contact who would pass their information further down the chain. For everyone's safety, they never knew who else was involved.

While Jake and his brothers were participating in anti-German activities, they never joined the more formal Dutch resistance. Their uncles were more involved, but Jake was never sure who he could trust. There were far too many people being betrayed to the Nazis. So Jake did most things with Neil and rarely participated in the planning and discussions of the larger resistance movement.

The Importance of a Cup of Coffee

As a miller, Jake was required to report all the grain that he milled. In addition, he was only allowed to mill for those who had a permit and then only for what that particular permit allowed. His farmer customers, like most others, felt that they could not survive within the ration system. They would keep some of their grain hidden from the Germans and then would bring it to Jake to grind it in secret. While Jake had an official set of books for the government controllers to review, he also had to keep track of the illegal orders that he received. Just to be safe, Jake usually got up early to do his illegal grinding and then would do the legitimate work during the day. In addition, when the controllers came, they usually came by boat and Jake would have plenty of warning to have everything in order for the inspection.

Early one morning when Jake and Neil were grinding, the inspectors showed up suddenly, without warning. As they were doing illegal grinding, Jake had his second record book with him, which the controllers promptly confiscated. This was a huge issue, as that book had all the names of the people who were participating in black market trading. At the very least, they would all be arrested and sent to the concentration camps. The controllers went into the house and Jake told Neil to "get that stuff out of here," referring to all the illegally milled flour. Jake then proceeded into the house and told his mother that the controllers had his book.

Instead of panicking, his mother offered the controllers a cup of coffee, a cup of real coffee. That was an unbelievable offer, as real coffee was almost non-existent in Germany and the Netherlands at that time. Since the German government had devoted all their resources to the war effort, they had long ago stopped importing coffee. It was very likely that this would be the first real cup of coffee these men had had in years. It was little surprise that they readily accepted.

They gathered around the kitchen table, put their papers on the table (along with Jake's book), and sat down to enjoy a wonderful cup of coffee. As they finished their first cup, Jake's mother asked, in her sweetest voice, if they would perhaps like another cup. They readily agreed. She went about cleaning the dishes from the table so that she could bring in a second round. As she was collecting the cups and saucers, she also slipped Jake's book into the mix. She proceeded to the kitchen, where she promptly threw the book into the wood stove. She then politely served the controllers their next round of coffee as if nothing had happened.

When they were finished, they got up and started looking for that book so they could proceed with the investigation. But the book was not to be found, and they started to get very angry. Jake's mother innocently asked if anything was wrong, but instead of answering, they stormed out to the mill to get the evidence that was there. Fortunately, Neil had ensured that it had all been removed, and he himself had also disappeared. Since Jake had been with them in the house the entire time, they couldn't accuse him of anything either. They left in a huff, empty-handed.

The Relatively Good Life

Given the conditions experienced by others during the war, the Van Seters family lived a relatively good life. Being in the milling business ensured that they had access to food, and it was particularly advantageous to have access to flour. From flour they could make bread, porridge, and pancakes. Jake also had a good relationship with some of the key farmers. He never gouged them, and they repaid his fairness by giving him a share of their produce.

Jake managed to take care of his family in several other ways. He had a friend make him a press so he could get oil out of oil seeds. As oil was scarce, this became a precious commodity for bartering. When Jake wanted to get engaged, he traded some of the oil he had made to a jeweler in Apeldoorn in exchange for engagement rings. He also bought one hundred kilograms of broken rice above and beyond what he needed for his animals. Rice was a good thing to stow away, as it kept for a very long time if it remained dry. Rice was especially good for people with weak stomachs, so it was also a good thing to have for bartering. In addition, Jake bought a lot of tobacco and cigarettes before they became restricted. Since he had the real stuff and not the terrible-smelling fake tobacco, he could command a premium price. In those days you could basically get whatever you wanted if you had tobacco.

While the Van Seters didn't have their freedom, they did not struggle to meet the basic needs that so many other people could not address. In spite of the relative comfort they enjoyed, they never found the situation normal. The ongoing presence of the Germans still tormented them, and they were determined to do what they could to fight against their Nazi oppressors.

They continued to risk their lives by hiding air force pilots and condemned Dutchmen.

Arrested without Cause

A few years into their occupation of the Netherlands, the Germans instituted a forced labour draft requiring able-bodied men over sixteen years old to go to work in Germany. Some exceptions were granted for essential skills, but these were very hard to obtain. When people who were summoned didn't show up, the Germans would conduct raids and send them forcibly. The German administration system was so thorough that they knew exactly how many people of each age group should have reported from each town. The problem was that most people really didn't want to go to Germany. They knew that the Germans would often put labourers in dangerous jobs, so that a lot of the people who went away never came back.

Both Jake and Neil tried very hard to obtain an exception, but they were unsuccessful. Neil went underground to avoid being sent away and resurfaced in Apeldoorn under an assumed identity as a twenty-six year old. Jake, however, was essential to the operation of the mill and therefore could not disappear. In the end his uncles were able to get the required documentation for him. Jake was not really sure whether these documents were forged or not, but he didn't really care; they seemed to suffice for a number of years. In all likelihood they were real documents that had been stolen as blanks and filled out later. In any case, they gave Jake a lot of mobility, to the point where he was able to go to Rotterdam every weekend to see his beloved Iet.

In early 1944, Neil got engaged to his girlfriend Mar and wanted to get married. At that time it wasn't clear how long the war would continue, so it didn't make much sense to Neil to wait. Neil and Mar set the date for May 24 in the town of Ulrum. Since he was in the wedding party, Jake arranged for someone else to manage the mill while he was gone. The family left on May 23, intending to pick up Iet in Rotterdam. As there were no passenger cars on the road anymore, they took a horse and buggy to the port on the island where they would catch a boat to Hellevoetsluis (a port town south of Rotterdam). They were so determined to get to the wedding on time that they left at 3:45 AM. When they got to the boat, their papers were checked, but just as before, there seemed to be no problem.

After the boat ride, the whole group took the train to Rotterdam and then caught a trolley to Maas Station to pick up Iet. The weather was beautiful, and everyone was looking forward to a very nice time. Jake thought Iet looked especially beautiful in the new dress that she had bought for the occasion.

Most of the party went directly to Ulrum, but Jake and Iet had to go to Apeldoorn to pick up another couple. They were first to travel to Utrecht and then transfer there. The nice chat they were having on the train was rudely interrupted by soldiers who asked for their identity papers. As this was not an unusual request, they handed them over. After the soldiers looked at the papers for a few minutes, one of them tucked the papers in an upper pocket and then they arrested Jake at gunpoint. They took him to a separate area of the train and guarded him there.

Strangely enough, Jake was the only person on that car who was apprehended. Normally, more people would have been taken. Also, the soldiers went directly to him without stopping to check the other passengers. It seemed like they were looking for him in particular.

While no one can be completely sure, to this day many people who knew Jake at that time believe that a neighbour who was a pro-Nazi sympathizer was responsible. They believe he had alerted the Germans to the fact that Jake was a trouble maker and that he would be traveling at that particular time. The family had always been wary of this particular individual, suspecting that he was feeding information to the Germans. While it was not unusual to be searched once in awhile, the Van Seters house was searched far more often than was normal. The circumstantial evidence is pretty overwhelming, but there was never any real proof, so this part of Jake's story remains a mystery.

Chapter 4: Imprisoned in the Netherlands

Once Jake was arrested, he asked what was going on and what he'd done wrong. The soldiers told him in German that he'd find out soon enough. They said they would tell him when they were good and ready, that it would be on their time, not his. He was never told why he was arrested. In fact, during his entire ordeal, he was never told why he was imprisoned or what he had done wrong. Once the Germans had him in custody, it didn't really seem to matter anymore.

Locked up in Filth

After he was arrested, Jake was first taken to Kamp Vught in the town of S'Hertogenbosch. This was one of the five main concentration camps in the Netherlands (the others being at Amersfoort, Westerbork, Ommen, and Schoorl). The camp operated from January 1943 to September 1944, with thirty thousand individuals passing through the camp during this time. Seven hundred forty-nine people lost their lives in Vught, although many more were killed in other camps once they'd been moved on from Vught.

The camp was divided into two main sections. One section was a local transit camp for Jews who were being sent to the extermination camps in Poland. Jews from the south of would first be collected at Kamp Vught, and then they were sent on to Westerbork, where they were combined with Jews from other parts of the Netherlands, before finally being were sent to Auschwitz-Birkenau, Sobibor, and other extermination camps. The other section of Vught was a security camp, where Dutch and Belgian political prisoners were held. It was in this second section that Jake was imprisoned.

Every account from prisoners who were interned at Kamp Vught paints a picture of a very primitive and disgusting place. The conditions there were terrible, disease was rampant, and there was a drastic shortage of food and water. The conditions were so bad that when certain Jewish children were sent from Vught to Westerbork, they were incredibly happy with the improvement. The abuse of prisoners at this camp was so severe that one camp commander, Adam Grünewald, was actually disciplined by Heinrich Himmler for being too brutal. He was demoted to the rank of regular soldier and was banished to the Hungarian front, where he died in 1945.[viii]

Jake's own recollection of the camp reinforces the accounts from other prisoners. When he arrived, they took his shoe laces, tie, belt, and suspenders. Then they unceremoniously dumped him into a cell that was barely larger than a square metre. The cell was dark, cold, damp, and smelled terrible. There was one rickety chair and a hole in the floor that served as the latrine. At night, the guards would take out the chair and put in a bag of straw for prisoners to sleep on. To make things even worse, the food was absolutely terrible and unfit for human consumption.

Jake only stayed in Kamp Vught for six days. No one told him why he was there, what he was charged with, or where he was going. He wasn't interrogated, and none of the guards ever talked to him. He was simply ignored. Jake had never been in prison, before so the sense of isolation was overwhelming. His only consolation at the time was that he still had some hope that the Dutch Underground would rescue him, so he was not completely in despair.

Kamp Vught was liberated by the Canadian forces in September of 1944, four months after Jake was there as a prisoner. As the Allies advanced, the Germans killed many of the remaining prisoners, executing 329 prisoners in the last few months of the camp's operation.

Today a World War II museum stands on a portion of the site that was occupied by Kamp Vught sixty years ago. Unfortunately, much of the original camp was torn down in the 1970s. The museum has managed to preserve one of the original barracks, the crematorium, and some of the fencing. They have also reconstructed a replica barrack to give visitors a good sense of what the camp would have been like at that time. With the resources at their disposal, the administration of Kamp Vught has done a remarkable job honouring the memories of those that died within its walls.

Upgraded to the Jail in Rotterdam

After spending six days in Kamp Vught, on May 30, 1944, Jake was sent to Rotterdam. He was transported by two Dutch couriers who had orders to kill him if he tried to escape. If Jake got away, their lives would be forfeit, so they took their duties seriously. They took him by train to the Maas Station in Rotterdam. Once he got onto the train platform, he was shocked and surprised to see his girlfriend Iet run up and put her arms around him. He had no idea that she even knew where he was, let alone that she would be at the train station. His mother and aunt were there as well. Apparently the members of the Dutch Underground had been tracking his movements and notified his family.

Jake's Dutch guards turned out to be decent men and told him that he could have an hour in a nearby park with Iet, as long as he promised not to escape. They assured him that if he attempted to run they would come after him and shoot him. So Jake swore to behave and went off with his girlfriend. The Underground had planned to rescue him there, but they never appeared. Even if they had shown up, they would have had to take Jake by force, as he was not about to break his word of his own volition. To Jake, if you give your word to someone, then you keep it. Otherwise you should not give your word in the first place. It was hard on both of them once the time was up, and Iet cried a lot. But she never suggested that he break his word and run away.

Once he went back to his guards, Jake was taken in a closed van to the Haagseveer police station. This was one of the few major buildings that had survived the bombing of Rotterdam intact. While intended to be a police station, it had largely been converted to a prison during the war and was now being used to hold political prisoners. The key purpose of this building was to facilitate the interrogation of prisoners before they were sent off to the concentration camps.

When Jake first got to Haagseveer, it was a big step up from Kamp Vught. Unlike Vught, it was relatively clean, didn't smell, and the food was far better. At first he had a lot more freedom. The guards even brought him small letters from family and friends, although they took them back once he had read them.

Unfortunately, the longer Jake stayed, the harsher the conditions became. He was promised that he could see his relatives, but that never happened. He was also taken off site several times to be questioned by experienced German interrogators. During these sessions, they tried every trick to get him to trip up and share information. They would ask strangely worded questions. They would dangle the promise of better treatment in exchange for information, and they would push to get Jake to betray other people who were "anti-German." They clearly didn't have anything concrete against him and were fishing for information. They were hoping Jake would make a mistake.

Even during these interrogations, Jake was treated better than most. He adopted several successful strategies. First, he always tried to get his interrogators talking. He felt that if they were busy talking, there would be a whole lot less hitting. Second, he played the role of the dumb country boy. When they pressed him to reveal names, he replied that given that he was so cut off from the rest of the world, he couldn't possibly know anything. He also asked a lot of questions. "Why am I here? What do you want from me? Is this how you'll accomplish your thousand-year Reich?" The only people Jake could have talked about if he had been so inclined were his two uncles who were involved in the resistance. But he never said a word, instead claiming that he was from a small, isolated island and that he knew nothing of the larger world.

When Jake was back in jail, a few of the other prisoners would try to befriend him. He never opened up to any of them, though. He always felt that the risk of a spy being planted among them was far too high. He mostly just kept to himself when he wasn't being interrogated. He was there for six weeks in June and July of 1944. Apart from the interrogations, his time in jail was extremely mundane and boring. But at least the place was clean and the food was decent.

While he was in Haagseveer, he received a message from the Dutch Underground that they had a plan to help him escape. The idea was to give him something that would make him seem very sick with a communicable disease. With such symptoms, it was pretty much guaranteed that Jake would be sent to the hospital. Once he was there, members of the underground would help him escape, as the hospitals did not have nearly the same level of security. Unfortunately, he was moved from Haagseveer before the plan could come together.

A few months after Jake left the Haagseveer prison, the Dutch Underground launched a raid of the prison. On October 25, 1944, led by Esmeijer Samuel, they managed to free forty-four of the men who were incarcerated there. The Germans retaliated by killing some of the prisoners who had not escaped. A few weeks later they arrested Esmeijer during another underground operation in Apeldoorn and subsequently executed him.[ix]

During the war, the Haagseveer prison was still largely run by Dutch nationals, who took orders directly from the Germans. There were 17,582 political prisoners who passed through the prison during the occupation. Most, like Jake, were eventually shipped to Kamp Amersfoort, but some of the Jews were sent directly to Westerbork.

The Haagseveer police station is still in operation today and is housed in the same building in downtown Rotterdam where Jake was held. The building has been extensively renovated over the years, but the basic architectural elements are still the same. While the building is a working police station and not a museum, there is a monument in the main entrance to the building commemorating all the political prisoners who were held there during the war, especially those who didn't survive.

The First Real Concentration Camp

It was early in July 1944 when Jake received notice to pack up his belongings. The time had come for him to leave the Haagseveer police station. Initially, he was very happy, as he thought he was going to be released. Up to this point, he had only been in jail (even the cell at Kamp Vught was more like a prison than a camp). He expected that he would soon be released, especially since the Germans hadn't actually charged him with anything or even told him why he was in trouble. Jake found out rather quickly that he was not being let go. Instead he was being transported to the concentration camp at Amersfoort. Again, the authorities did not tell him why he was being sent there or how long he would have to stay.

When he arrived at the new camp, Jake realized that things had gotten much more serious. Amersfoort was a much better organized and well-secured location. There was virtually no chance of escape or rescue. While there weren't many more guards at Amersfoort than at the other locations, they were much more effective. They had high observation towers, and there were several rows of high fences (with at least one being an electric fence).

Prisoners who tried to escape from Amersfoort were shot on sight or if they survived, were hung in the main courtyard as a warning to others. The guards received two bonus days off for shooting an escapee. The more sadistic among them would lure prisoners toward the fences by throwing cigarettes just on the inside of the fence. When the prisoners went to retrieve them, the guards would claim that the prisoners were trying to escape and would shoot them.

Once prisoners got to the camp they had to go through a rigorous induction process. For the first time Jake was given a prisoner number: 2047. From then on he was only referred to by his number and never his name. He was stripped of all his personal possessions, including his clothes and jewelry. He then had to march completely naked to another building about one hundred metres away to get a new wardrobe.

The prisoners were given old clothes from dead Dutch soldiers. The clothes were full of holes, stank incredibly, and were infested with vermin. Jake ended up with long johns that were really only legs, a decent undershirt, a pair of pants with no crotch, and an infested jacket that only had one button. The next step of the process for the prisoners was having their heads shaved. Most prisoners also had their shoes taken away and were forced to walk around in wooden clogs. These clogs were not the brightly painted souvenirs that one finds in the tourist shops in Amsterdam, but rather they were crude, roughly hewn pieces of wood that only vaguely resembled shoes. This worried Jake more than anything, as he couldn't walk in clogs. He was convinced that if he had to wear the clogs he wouldn't survive for long. Fortunately, they didn't have any clogs in his size and he was allowed to keep the shoes he had.

The whole process of induction into Kamp Amersfoort was geared to psychologically break the prisoner's spirit and remove his or her identity. The process that Jake went through was not an isolated event; this was standard practice at the camp. When the prisoners arrived, they all had their own individual style and appearance. Once the camp administration was done with them, they all looked the same, stripped of their individuality. The Nazis believed that people without an identity were far less likely to rebel and far more likely to follow orders from the camp commanders, like mute sheep.

Jake found this one of the hardest parts of his ordeal, being treated more as an animal than as a person. He remembers looking at himself in the mirror with his ratty clothes and his shaved head and feeling very sorry for himself. In a period of just over six weeks, he had lost everything. He had been taken from his family, he had been stripped of his possessions, and he'd lost all his clothes. Even more important, he'd lost whatever freedom he had living in occupied Netherlands and was now stuck in a concentration camp for an indefinite period of time. He also realized that if the Germans had taken him through this kind of indoctrination, there was a very high likelihood that he would be incarcerated for a much longer period than he had first believed.

In his book *Survival in Auschwitz*, Primo Levi talks about the effects this process had on him:

> Then, for the first time, we became aware that our language lacks words to express this offence, the demolition of a man. In a moment, with almost prophetic intuition, the reality was revealed to us: we had reached the bottom. It is not possible to sink lower than this; no human condition is more miserable than this, nor could it conceivably be so. Nothing belongs to us anymore. They have taken away our clothes, our shoes, even our hair. If we speak, they will not listen to us, and if they listen, they will not understand. They will even take away our name.[x]

There was another major difference between Amersfoort and the previous places he had been imprisoned. In Vught and Haagseveer, he was left to languish in his cell all day. In Amersfoort there was much more that had to be done. For instance, all the prisoners had to march around on parade three times a day, with each march lasting from sixty to ninety minutes. The first parade was at five o'clock in the morning and the last one at nine o'clock at night. The marches were so strenuous that people would regularly collapse. While Jake made it through all the marches, at the end of the day he would have badly blistered feet, even with the shoes he had been allowed to keep. To this day he is convinced that he wouldn't have survived one march on wooden shoes.

During each parade the prisoners had to stand at attention while their numbers were called out. This was done so that everyone could be counted and the guards could ensure that no one had escaped that day. This process required all the prisoners to stand at absolute attention for a long period of time. If anyone fell out of line, he or she was beaten severely. The only lasting physical effect that Jake retained from his time in captivity was as a result of these marches. He suffered nerve damage to his leg as a result of standing at attention for such long periods of time.

Besides marching, all the prisoners were required to work throughout the day. There were several choices of activities. One group was doing calisthenics, and Jake thought that would be one of the easier things to do. He was proven wrong, as the workouts were so intense that the next day every muscle in his body ached with pain. He was sure there was no way he was going to survive if he had to do that every day, so he decided to switch to another activity. Jake had seen that a group was weaving straw, and again he thought that it looked quite easy, but it too was not nearly as simple as it seemed. Each person had to weave one hundred metres of straw mat each day, whether they knew how to weave or not. If a prisoner didn't make the quota, he or she was punished quite severely. Jake and the prisoners with him wove like mad all day and came nowhere near making their quota. They managed to get only thirty-five metres finished. Knowing that he was going to get punished, Jake had to come up with a creative solution. He found out where the finished straw was kept and managed to steal a roll. While it was very dangerous and he probably would have been shot if he had been caught, he really didn't feel like he had much of a choice. For the rest of his time at Amersfoort, Jake continued to hand in stolen rolls of woven straw. As a result, he was largely left alone.

Historically Kamp Amersfoort (or Polizeiliches Durrchgangslager Amersfoort, as it was also known) stood out among the camps in the Netherlands for the particularly cruel activities that occurred there. The camp was run by a sadistic German named Joseph Kotella, a man who in 1938 had been diagnosed as mentally unstable. Kotella had the guards use the camp shooting range as an execution ground for dozens of Russian soldiers, who were then dumped in mass, unmarked graves. And it was Kotella who came up with the infamous Rose Garden of Kamp Amersfoort. This was a rectangular-shaped area in the middle of the main courtyard that was surrounded by barbed wire. Prisoners who were being punished had to stand still and erect in this area for twenty-four or forty-eight hours. They had no food or water and were not allowed to sit down. Anyone who has had to stand at attention for a long period of time can attest to how incredibility painful this type of treatment can be. While Jake never did get the full rose garden treatment, he did have to march and stand at attention for periods of up to eight hours. As a result of all of his barbaric behavior, Kotella was executed by the Dutch government shortly after the war ended.[xi]

The food at Amersfoort was terrible and nutritionally inadequate. Another Dutch prisoner who was in Amersfoort at the time, a man named Van Dierman, recalls that the daily rations existed of "half a litre of watery soup, some turnips, and three slices of bread." Van Dierman himself lost thirty pounds while at camp. He later commented that after anyone had been at the camp for a while, he or she looked like a walking skeleton.

The only real positive element at Amersfoort was the presence of the Red Cross. When they came around for inspections, all the Germans were on their best behavior. The Germans kept the camp in much better shape overall because they were being watched. The Red Cross gave out care packs to all the prisoners, consisting of soap and some food. The prisoners appreciated these packages very much, as it was the only time they would get these kinds of supplies. The only rule the Germans had was that the Red Cross workers could not talk to the prisoners, as the Germans feared that the Red Cross personnel would be used to pass messages to and from the inmates.

It was while he was at Amersfoort that Jake and the other prisoners heard of the Allied landing at Normandy. The attack on French soil had happened on June 6, while he was in Rotterdam, but Jake had little access to that type of information from inside the prison. While the news lifted the prisoners' spirits a little, the fact that they had heard so much propaganda from both sides made it difficult for them to know if there was much substance to the reports. The outcome of the war was definitely shifting in favour of the Allied forces, but little evidence of this was seen or heard within the camps.

Once Jake had been at Amersfoort for a week, he was told that he was getting transported to Germany. This was not completely unexpected, as

Amersfoort was mainly operated as a transit camp where prisoners were held before they were moved to other locations. He was allowed to send a letter to his family telling them he was going to Germany. They were also allowed to bring him one suitcase and a letter.

The challenge for his family was that there were no suitcases to be had in the Netherlands during the war, so they went to a local carpenter and had him make a suitcase out of wood. While it did the job when it came to carrying Jake's possessions, it was extremely heavy. It was also very large, measuring over one foot high, two feet wide, and three feet long.

The fact that Jake was feeling sorry for himself didn't stop him from standing up for his rights. The day before he was meant to leave for Germany, the guards were under order to give the prisoners back their personal possessions, but individual guards were stealing the more valuable items, including Jake's gold ring and his watch. He had just gotten engaged to Iet, so the ring in particular was very valuable to him. The prisoners had to sign a piece of paper stating they had not been mistreated and that their property had been returned to them. When it was his turn, Jake refused to sign. That was a problem for the guards, as all the paperwork had to be in order or else they would get in trouble. They threatened to shoot him if he didn't sign. "Go ahead," he said. He was pretty confident that shooting him would just have caused more problems for the guards. When he insisted on speaking to the camp commandant, they relented and gave him back his watch and ring. While he would later have to trade the watch for food, he kept that ring for the entire time he was imprisoned and still has it to this day.

Kamp Amersfoort was reopened as a museum/memorial in 2005. While most of the original camp is gone, the administrators retained one of the original guard towers (unlike those at Kamp Vught, which are all replicas). Visitors can also see the shooting range where so many Russian soldiers are buried, as well as "The Stone Man" statue that appears on the cover of this book.

Shipped off to Germany

While Jake knew he was going to Germany, he did not anticipate how it would happen. It was two o'clock in the morning on July 20 when about four hundred men in Amersfoort were told to get their things together in order to leave. The SS guards were unusually agitated, and all the prisoners had to run from the camp to the train station. It was a dark night, and the prisoners had to run between rows of SS guards. As the prisoners went by, the guards began randomly beating and even shooting some of people running by. It was one of the most terrifying events that Jake had ever experienced. It didn't help that he had to carry that heavy wooden suitcase for the entire distance that they had to run (the train station was 2.6 kilometres from the camp). By the time he got to the train station, he was as tired as he had ever been in his life. Even today he's still not quite sure how he made it, but he was on the train when it left at four o'clock.

When he got to the train station at the Dutch border town of Hengelo, Jake got an even bigger shock. The Dutch underground had continued to track his movements and had alerted his family exactly when he was being sent to Germany. They had come to this particular station to see if they could find him. As the train pulled into the station, Jake looked out to see his mother and his girlfriend there waiting for him. He banged on the window, and they looked right at him. They didn't recognize him. It had only been two months, but with the maltreatment and his shaved head, even his own mother couldn't really tell it was him.

Eventually his family realized who he was and tried to bring him some of the food and cigarettes they had brought for him. But the Nazi guards were ruthless and would not let them near the train. The whole platform was cordoned off by the Germans. The train slowly pulled out of the station, leaving his family behind. To be that close to them and not get to see or talk to them hurt Jake deeply. Today he can still clearly remember the wave of emotion that passed over him as he left them behind. He wouldn't see or even have contact with them for another eleven months.

The German Camp System

There were four different kinds of camps in the German camp system; transit camps, concentration camps, extermination camps, and slave labour camps. While each served a specific purpose, there was overlap in the camps. Some camps served as both labour and extermination camps, while others were both concentration and transit camps.

Kamp Vught, Kamp Amersfoort, and Kamp Westerbork were all transit camps. The transit camps were mostly located in Western Europe, and their purpose was to aggregate and move people on to other camps as quickly and efficiently as possible. They were part of a carefully planned system that allowed the Nazis to efficiently relocate millions of people during the war.

While the Jews were the primary target, most people from occupied countries who ended up in Germany also passed through a transit camp on the way to their final destination.[xii]

The second type of camp was the concentration camp. While this term is also sometimes used to refer to any of the camps, the concentration camp was really the long-term prison camp for anyone the Nazi regime didn't want causing trouble. They were typically full of political prisoners, captured prisoners of war, and anyone else the Nazis found to be a nuisance (Jehovah's Witnesses, religious opponents, members of the press, etc). While these camps frequently had some sort of extermination facilities, their main purpose was to hold people in detention. Some famous examples of concentration camps are Buchenwald, Bergen-Belsen, Dachau, and Ravensbruck. A lot of these camps were quite large and could hold tens of thousands of people. As an example, the women's camp at Ravensbruck had a capacity of twenty thousand. Buchenwald, a massive camp located near the Nazi stronghold of Weimar, held up to one hundred and twelve thousand people.[xiii]

The extermination camps are the most infamous of the different types of camps, undoubtedly because it was at these camps that the worst atrocities occurred. The main purpose of these camps was to exterminate whole groups of people as quickly and efficiently as possible. While the Jewish people were the main group targeted for extermination, other groups such as gypsies, homosexuals, and communists often met similar fates. The most well-known of these camps was the dual camp of Auschwitz-Birkenau. While slightly less famous, the camps of Treblinka, Sobibor, and Belzec were also major extermination centres. Most of the extermination camps were located in Poland, as the Nazis did not want to conduct their dirty business in their own backyard.[xiv]

The fourth type of camp, the slave labour camp, is by far the least known and understood of the camps in the German system. While most people can name one of the extermination camps and many can name a concentration camp, very few can name any of the work camps. Most people don't even know that they existed, and it's not because there were so few of these camps. During the war, there were over two hundred slave labour camps in Germany alone, making them by far the most common type of camp that existed.[xv] The Brinnlitz camp run by Oskar Schindler, the man made famous in the movie *Schindler's List*, fit within this slave labour camp category.

There are many reasons why the slave labour camps are less well known. They were typically smaller, so they did not gain the same level of notoriety. Since they did not typically kill large numbers of their inmates outright, they did not cause the same level of moral outrage. Instead, they slowly worked people to death and then replaced them with new prisoners. But perhaps the most important reason they are less well known is that the Nazis and the companies who used them purposely tried to hide them and deny their existence during the war. Though Jake didn't know much about these camps while he was still in the Netherlands, he would become very well acquainted with them during his eleven-month stay in Germany.

Feeding the War Machine

It was not an accident that Jake ended up being sent to Germany. As much as it may have seemed to him at the time to be a series of random events, his arrest was part of a larger, coordinated effort to get additional labourers into Germany, especially as the outcome of the war hung in the balance. While he was arrested in 1944, the policies that led to his arrest had been put in place years earlier.

The challenge that the Germans had from the very beginning of the war is that they did not have sufficient people to both build up their army and to run their industries. Given that most German men had been conscripted into the army, there was a serious lack of people to run the German industrial system. That was a major problem, as without the steel, munitions, and most importantly fuel that these industries produced, the Nazi war machine would come to a grinding halt. While the Germans could easily extract the raw materials from the countries they conquered, obtaining the necessary labour was a more difficult problem.

In World War I, Germany had largely solved their labour problem by recruiting women into the workforce. But by the start of World War II, this option was less appealing. The culture in Germany had changed, and there would have been significant resistance to such a policy. The well-publicized and accepted cultural model for a woman in Nazi Germany was to be "the mother of the nation." Biological reproduction and cultural reinforcement were promoted as the key responsibilities for women. The idea of women making bombs simply did not fit with Nazi ideology and propaganda. Some within the Nazi party realized the flaw in this model and managed to get a law passed that authorized the conscription of women. Even though it was official, it was never enforced, and women continued in their domestic roles. In contrast, the United States was very successful in recruiting women into their workforce, one of the factors that allowed them to ramp up their wartime manufacturing so dramatically.

While employing women was not seen as a viable option, there were also major concerns that importing foreign workers would affect the German bloodlines. The last thing many Nazi leaders wanted was "inferior" people such as the Poles, Ukrainians, or Greeks adversely affecting their vision of the Aryan nation.[xvi]

The labour shortage became even worse when the German Blitzkrieg stalled in its assault on Russia in 1941. German industry had been counting on the rapid return of their regular workers from the front lines when the army won quickly and decisively, but this possibility grew more and more remote as the war on the eastern front started to drag on. The employees that German companies had been relying on were stuck on the front lines, unable to return home.

The answer the Nazi officials chose was to use forced slave labour from the countries they conquered, a program known as the Auslander-Einstatz (the deployment of foreigners). They decided that the program was the lesser evil, especially when laws could be put in place outlawing inter-racial communications. After a successful pilot program with three hundred thousand Polish workers, the Germans launched programs to conscript labour from all the countries they had conquered.[xvii]

From 1942 until the end of the war, the German economy was almost completely dependent on slave labour. Without their imported workforce, the Germans would never have been able to maintain the level of agricultural and munitions production that they needed throughout the war. With their slave labour, the Germans maintained the highest level of per capita food production of any of the combatant European countries.

By 1944, they had imported workers from twenty European countries. Foreigners now made up 26 percent of the overall employed workforce in Germany. There were over seven million foreign labourers in Germany during the war, three hundred fifty thousand of whom were Dutch. These resources were used in all sectors of the economy but were especially prevalent in the low-skilled, blue-collar jobs. While many of the companies that used slave labour in Germany are long gone, current industry giants such as BMW, Volkswagen, and Siemens all participated extensively.[xviii]

In 1944, the Nazis found that even their forced conscription was not meeting all their needs, so they began to use the inmates in concentration camps as labourers. Concentration camps would loan groups of five hundred prisoners to companies and would move those prisoners to subsidiary camps located near the businesses. For a nominal fee, the companies could greatly increase their work forces. To keep the camps full, the Nazi SS looked for any excuse to arrest the remaining able- bodied individuals and send them back to Germany. The Nazis got so desperate for labour, they started using Jewish workers, an idea they would not even have considered a few years earlier.

Unfortunately for the foreigners, there was another policy concerning slave labourers. The Nazis had a principle called "Venichtung durch Arbeit" or "Extermination through Labour." This principle led to slave labourers being given only the minimal amount of food and only the most basic tools. It was still cheaper for the Nazis to go find new slave labourers than it was to take proper care of the ones they had. Once a worker was worn out, he or she would simply be exterminated and replaced.[xix]

In the book *Less than Slaves*, Benjamin Ferencz documents the testimony of one of the Jewish slave labourers who was specifically told by a plant foreman that they were being deliberately worked to death.[xx] This foreman was employed by the same company and was likely at the same factory where Jake would later find himself imprisoned.

The Importance of Synthetic Fuel

Synthetic fuel ended up playing a very large role in the rise and the fall of the Nazi movement. The challenge Germany faced at the beginning of the war was that their yearly requirements of 44 million barrels of oil far outweighed their domestic supply of only 3.8 million barrels of traditional oil. Before the war began, they were importing 28 million barrels from overseas and 3.8 million barrels overland from their neighbours and were producing a further 9 million barrels through synthetic means like the coal extraction method (there were a few other methods that were used as well). As they had found out in World War I, they could quickly lose their overseas supply if the Allied forces implemented a naval blockade.

Faced with uncertain supplies, the Germans had to come up with other ways of fulfilling their fuel requirements. They used a multi-pronged strategy to fill the gap. First, partially helped by their annexation of Austria, they increased their domestic production of oil from 3.8 million barrels to 12 million barrels per year. They also captured the oil supplies of other countries they invaded in Blitzkrieg fashion, adding 10 million barrels of oil to their stockpiles. Those numbers left them far short of their wartime requirements.

Their initial solution long-term had been to attack Russia and gain access to the 220 million barrels of oil produced annually in the Caucasian region of that country. The Russians had other ideas, however, and put up a valiant resistance. The Germans were successful in capturing the smallest of the three major oil fields but were never able to capture the other two larger fields. Even though they were losing control of one of their oil fields, the Russians were not about to let all those reserves fall into German hands. In the tradition of their scorched earth approach to defending their country, the Russians so badly damaged the facilities at the field they lost that Germans were never able to extract any of the oil.

Since the Germans were unable to capture sufficient supplies of traditional oil, as the war progressed, the strategy of utilizing synthetically produced fuel took on a much greater importance. If there Germans were to win the war, they would need to drastically improve on the 9 million barrels of synthetic oil they were producing.

Earlier in 1934, the Minister of Economics in Germany, a man by the name of Schacht, had begun initiatives to ensure Germany could be self-supporting in a number of essential materials. The most important of these was gasoline to power the German Bleitzkreig. He "encouraged" the ten existing lignite producing companies to merge to form the Braunkohlen-Benzin AG (BRABAG) organization and then compelled them to focus their efforts on fuel production. With the help of technology from the United States, the BRABAG organization started producing gasoline from the plentiful supplies of brown coal found in the eastern regions of Germany.[xxi]

The process of making synthetic fuel consisted of heating the coal, extracting the tars and oils found inside, and then distilling the resulting liquid into fuel. The problem with the process was that it was very inefficient. It took a very large amount of coal to create the necessary tars and oils. Once these were distilled, only 10 percent of the remaining product was of high enough quality to be used as gasoline. The remaining 90 percent had to be used as diesel or heating oil. While these inefficiencies have kept coal-derived gasoline from being a significant force in the post-war economy, at the time Germany had little choice but to rely on this process.

The only other country that subsequently used the synthetic fuel technology to a great extent was South Africa during its apartheid years. That country was also cut off from other sources and needed to find ways of running its economy without the import of overseas oil.[xxii]

By 1943, the Germans had used up much of their captured stockpiles and were almost entirely reliant on their own direct production. They had successfully increased production of synthetic fuels from the prewar levels of 9 million barrels a year to 36 million barrels per year through expanding existing facilities and building new factories. The role that synthetic fuels now played in Germany increased from 22 percent of the total supply to more than 50 percent. This increased reliance on synthetic fuels was one of the main reasons Jake was sent to Germany as a slave labourer. The Germans simply did not have enough domestic labour to run all the production facilities on their own. Not surprisingly, given the reliance the German Army had on synthetic fuels, the factories producing these fuels became the most important bombing targets for the Allied air forces.

Chapter 5: Surviving the Labour Camps

After leaving Amersfoort, Jake spent the next seven hours traveling across Germany in a packed box car. The train finally arrived in the town of Espenhain, a small community about twenty kilometres south of Leipzig. The ride was excruciatingly hot, and the prisoners could not open any of the windows, so they were faint with thirst. As soon as they got off the train, they made a mad dash for the nearest tap, even though they had been warned that they could contract typhoid from the water. No sooner had they quenched their thirst than the prisoners were handed to a group of guards and taken to their new home—a slave labour camp supporting the local factory complex in Espenhain.

The German Factory Camps

As discussed in the previous chapter, Germany had become reliant on slave labour to feed its war machine. The use of these slave labourers posed a bit of a problem. The German companies who ran the industry were used to having willing employees, not unwilling, seditious slave labourers. To help ensure the system functioned properly, the Nazis built slave labour camps and assigned guards to keep the workers in line. The German name for these camps was Arbeitserziehungslager, which literally translates to "workers education camps." The term education camp referred to the fact that their official role was to be reform camps for troublesome workers, who could then be educated in the proper ways of industry. Many of the camps even had slogans such as "Freedom through Work," much like the infamous gate at the entrance of Auschwitz. As a result, the labour camps were not built in a luxurious manner. Rather, the official policy was that they were to have conditions more severe than the concentration camps.[xxiii]

There were over two hundred of these camps in Germany during the Second World War. The camps were operated as sub-camps to the larger concentration camps. The largest network of camps was run by the administration of the Buchenwald concentration camp. This network, comprising of 140 sub-camps located around Germany, included the camp Böhlen where Jake would later end up.[xxiv] The large concentration camps would supply the SS guards needed to run the company camps. They would also arrange for a steady flow of prisoners to the camps, ensuring there were new workers to replace those that had been "used up."

When the labour camps were first opened, the intention was that people would not stay for more than two months, so the harsh conditions would be manageable. As the war went on, the type of people changed and the length they stayed increased, but the conditions never really improved. The typical work schedule was twelve hours a day, seven days a week. A normal day consisted of getting up at 4:30 for parade, then off to work by 5:30, with the work day lasting from 6:00 AM until 6:00 PM. Two months in one of the labour camps reduced a man to skin and bones. It was not uncommon for men to lose forty kilograms in those first two months.

The camp in Espenhain where Jake found himself was built to support an industrial complex that consisted of a chemical factory and a power station. They both were built between 1937 and 1942 to support Germany's war efforts by producing the necessary fuel for the German army and air force. There was also another larger factory complex located five kilometres down the road in the town of Böhlen. The buildings there had been constructed a few years earlier. Both locations had been part of a company called Aktiengesellschaft Sächsische Werke (ASW) but were merged into the larger BRABAG organization in 1934. BRABAG became one of the largest users of slave labour in Germany.[xxv]

While it was hard to keep track of time while at the factory camps, Jake believes that he was in the camp at Espenhain from July to sometime in December of 1944. The camp was quite small. When Jake arrived, there were about three hundred people located there. The Germans told the prisoners that they were in a "protected" camp, so they couldn't do whatever they wanted. The camp administrators insisted that they didn't want anyone along for a free ride but that people had to work for their keep. They promised that if the prisoners did good work, they would have a good life and maybe they'd be set free. In this way, they gave the prisoners a glimmer of hope. On the other hand, they also were very clear that they would shoot anyone who tried to escape. Unfortunately, the camp guards were not so good at keeping the first promise, but they were very effective at keeping the second one.

To ensure that the local guards were extra vigilant with the slave labourers, the camp administrators lied to them about how the slave labourers were very dangerous. The guards were told that the prisoners had killed or tried to kill German soldiers, and that that's why they were imprisoned. But they never mentioned to the prisoners what they had told the guards. As a result, the slave labourers were treated as dangerous criminals without having any clue as to what precipitated such treatment.

When people arrived, they were supposed to be ready to work, but most had hardly anything to wear anymore, so the camp administrators gave them better clothes to work in. So at first there seemed to be some improvement, at least compared to what they had before. The prisoners also received wooden klompen (half shoe/half wood) like the ones they had been issued in the Netherlands. But Jake still had his shoes, and fortunately they didn't take those away from him.

When the guards took the prisoners into the camp, they gave the new slave labourers a place where they could sleep and a sack with some straw they could lay on. While not a soft mattress, it was still better than sleeping on the floor. Thirty men were assigned to each room, and with a lot of juggling and squeezing, they managed to lie down. They were barely on the ground when some of the guards entered the room. All the slave labourers jumped up as they had been trained to do in Amersfoort. The Germans indicated that wasn't necessary and that the prisoners could lie down again. They merely counted the labourers and left.

The guards had barely walked out when suddenly the lights went out and the air raid siren began. The new arrivals were terrified at first, as most had not been through such an experience. They asked if there were bombs shelters, but upon finding that there were none, they went back to their beds.

While the discipline was fairly lax on the first day in camp, the next day things changed and the easy life was over. In the morning, and every morning after that, the men had to get up at 3:30, show up for parade drill for an hour, and then start work at 6:00 AM. There were three guards with rifles, and if a person did not work hard enough to please them, one of the guards would hit him with the butt of their rifle. Initially, the slave labourers were given a break from 9:00 to 9:30, but that was discontinued. They did get a break from 1:00 to 1:30, and that break was kept. They worked until 6:00 and then returned to camp. They had to march again for an hour, line up for the parade, and then finally, at approximately 7:30, they received their first and only meal of the day. It consisted of two slices of bread and a litre of watery cabbage soup.

At the end of the day they dragged their tired, skeletal bodies back to the straw sacks and collapsed in total exhaustion.

When they first arrived, the slave labourers were quartered in three barracks, but after a few months, one had to be vacated, leaving only two. These were already filled to capacity, which meant that a number of men had to sleep outside. While these conditions were already bad, things were about to get worse.

The guards moved the slave labourers into new quarters again. This time the prisoners were in a large room that they had to share with about three hundred men. Their previous quarters had been re-assigned to Russian prisoners of war. In this new room, there was only some straw spread on the ground, and that was all they had to sleep on. They had no light at night, and everything was dirty and infested with vermin. The slave labourers were left with one tap for washing and only one toilet, even though more than half of the men were suffering from diarrhea. If someone wanted to use that toilet, he had to wait around for at least an hour, if he could manage.

Sometime in December of 1944, Jake was relocated to the camp at Böhlen, located five kilometres down the road from Espenhain. He would stay there until April of 1945. He remembers the camps as being quite different. The camp at Böhlen was much larger (perhaps about fifteen hundred labourers) and was much better organized. While some of the work at Espenhain had seemed unstructured, mundane, and even pointless, the administration was far more organized and efficient at Böhlen.

At both places the camp administrators interviewed each worker to as to the skills he had. They wrote everything down, and then put the slave labourers into groups. Sometimes they needed certain skills (carpenters, welders, etc) when there was a big shortage. If a prisoner put up his hand, the guards generally just put him in that group without checking their records or certifications. Jake went from one job to another, even though he had no actual qualifications for many of his "volunteer" positions.

On one occasion Jake signed up to work on fixing a cement mixer that the Germans couldn't get going. As many of the other jobs that involved very heavy work, Jake thought that working on a cement mixer would be relatively light, so he told them he was used to working on that type of machine. This story was actually not a complete fabrication, given that he had to fix his own diesel engine in the mill. While he knew something about machinery, he was still very fortunate to get the mixer working. While he was fixing things, he also tried to sabotage them so they would break again in the future. In the case of the cement mixer, he put a little sand in the oil so that it would seize up. Even though he was a prisoner, he still felt compelled to do what he could to slow the German war machine.

Another time Jake volunteered to cut up steel that had been damaged in a recent bombing attack. This time he had absolutely no experience and could not figure out how to get the cutting torch to work. When the German guards confronted him, he claimed that he had only had experience with the machines in the Netherlands and that they were totally different. The guards believed him and showed him how to use the equipment.

One job Jake didn't mind was working on the anti-aircraft guns. This work consisted of using cement to repair the foundations around the guns that had been damaged in bombings. Since these guns were located a fair distance away from the factory, the slave labourers needed to be transported there. Once they got to the location, they were guarded by the army that was stationed there, not by the SS who guarded them at the camp. The army was made up of much more normal, caring people than the SS. The soldiers were much friendlier and took better care of the slave labourers than the camps guards ever did.

The worst job for the prisoners came after the allied forces had bombed the factory. The Germans needed everything up and running as soon as possible, so they pushed the slave labourers to get all the debris moved out. Some of that debris was very heavy, and the Germans were always in a great hurry to get it removed, as they wanted everything fixed as soon as possible. They would drive the slave labourers hard, but it was never good enough or never fast enough. The Germans also devised an effective way to ensure that everyone worked their hardest. All ten wheelbarrows that were used had to be full of debris at the same time, and those who fell behind would be beaten. There were always some who were scared and worked hard; consequently, the rest were forced to keep up to their pace.

Aside from these intermittent jobs, the main task Jake performed was working in the coal mines. There were open pit mines around both Espenhain and Böhlen, and Jake had to work extracting coal from the horizontal shafts in the mine. There were tracks along the floor on which the slave labourers had to push mining carts in and out of the shafts. The shafts were small and dark and only had one entrance. If they collapsed during a bombing attack, the people inside would be trapped forever. The mines really weren't the healthiest place to begin with, as they were constantly wet and cold. A lot of people who worked in them would become quite sick. So Jake would do whatever he could to get away from mine duty.

When the prisoners first arrived at the camp, they had received a crudely made bowl and cutlery for their meals. Unfortunately, the food was similar to

Kamp Amersfoort, with the basic daily diet consisting of a slice of bread and watery soup. As per German policy, the amount of food was simply not enough to sustain the slave labourers, and many of them died due to malnutrition and starvation. The food situation was so bad that the camp commandant at Böhlen, upon receiving a transport of one thousand men from Buchenwald, sent a message back warning against sending more slave labourers to him. It was not that he didn't have the work, but rather he didn't have enough food to keep them all alive.

Jake recalls that people in the camps died from a combination of hunger and misery. From the hunger perspective, anytime anyone in the camp stopped eating, the rest of the inmates knew he was finished. The final step in malnutrition and starvation is that the body starts rejecting food and a person's hunger disappears. Prisoners would also just give up hope and would die shortly thereafter. The slave labourers became so used to death that when they saw someone who was following that predictable path, they would callously tell him that he would probably be dead tomorrow. While this may seem harsh, the circumstances they lived in deadened their feelings of concern and empathy. In *Man's Search for Meaning* Viktor Frankl talks about a similar process that occurred during his time in Auschwitz:

> One after another the members of the little community in our hut died. Each of us could calculate with fair accuracy whose turn would be next, and when his own would come. After many observations we knew the symptoms quite well, which made the correctness of our prognosis quite certain. "He won't last long," or, "This one is the next one," we would whisper to each other.[xxvi]

By Jake's observation, the older inmates were the first to go. They simply did not have the strength required to put up with the demanding work or the abuse from the guards. The next were those who were married and had families. While in theory they had much to live for, the added pressure of worrying about their families was often more than they could bear. It was the young single ones like Jake that seemed to survive the longest, although that was more of a general observation than a hard rule. Jake remembers people who looked healthy and fit but died very quickly. He also remembers those who he was sure were going to die but who would somehow pull through.

There was one survivor in particular that really surprised Jake. Of the few friends he did make in Böhlen, one was named Wilhelm Sculeman. When Jake had last seen him at the camp he had looked like a walking dead person. He had refused to give up even though there was almost nothing left of him. When the Allied troops finally found him, William had tuberculosis and was at the point of death. He had to spend a year in a hospital in Switzerland to recover from his ordeal. But he did recover, and one day, he called Jake up and told him that he wanted to come to Jake's hometown of Dirksland for a visit. Jake was completely surprised, as he had long assumed that William had died in the camp, like so many others in his position. When the visit occurred, Jake's fiancé thought that William was incredibly skinny. But to Jake he looked very fat, especially compared to what he had been before.

The slave labourers had very little interaction with the normal factory workers. A factory foreman would come and tell them what to do and then their guards would stay with them to ensure they did it and that they didn't try to escape. The factory workers themselves were often from other countries, although they had been brought in through less forcible means. As an example, the foreman at the factory was an older man from Czechoslovakia.

While there are many records confirming the existence of the camp at Böhlen, (also known as Böhlen-Peres or Peres-Lippendorf, after some of the other small towns in the area), there are fewer readily available records that discuss a separate camp at Espenhain. Even within the records located at the Buchenwald concentration camp, Espenhain is not mentioned, nor is it shown on the map of sub-camps. There is, however, firsthand testimony from other Dutch prisoners confirming that they were also sent to the camp at Espenhain. Some of them even managed to hold on to their identification from the camp, proving that it did actually exist. Perhaps, given its proximity to the Böhlen camp, it was actually part of the same camp operation. Or perhaps it was simply too small of a camp and therefore was not worth documenting.

After the war, both Espenhain and Böhlen were briefly in the hands of the Americans. But both were also physically located in the territory that had been promised to the Russians. So the Americans left, and the Russians took over in August of 1945. They rebuilt the destroyed factories and continued to use the camps as detainment centres well into the 1980s.

If you go to Espenhain today, you will find that almost all reminders of the war period are gone. There is no trace of the camp, and most of the war-era buildings have been torn down. The main buildings of the industrial complex were torn down in 1990 to make way for a new industrial park development. There are only a handful of the old World War II era buildings left. And in the place where the coal piles used to stand, the Germans have built one of the world's largest solar power plants (five megawatts). Apparently the ground was too polluted to be used for anything else.

If you go to Böhlen, the story is similar. Most of the buildings from the original factory complex are gone. The only remaining structures are a few old brick buildings and one of the factory smoke stacks. In place of the rest of the complex, there is now a Dow Chemical factory and the massive Lippendorf coal power plant (1840 megawatts). The original location of the factory camp where the slave labourers were held is an unmarked area just south of the power plant.

The town of Böhlen still has a very industrial feel to it. There are still many cold war era buildings, and no matter where you are in the town, you can see the huge cooling towers from the nearby power plant. There is one key difference between Espenhain and Böhlen. Next to the main gate of the Dow chemical plant just outside of Böhlen, there is a grassy area in front of a brick wall. In front of the brick wall are two monuments, and on the wall are several plaques. These are memorials to the people who suffered and died in the Böhlen camp. For Jake, the most important and moving of these memorials is the large stone monument that commemorates the suffering and death of Dutch nationals who were enslaved there. He realizes that only by God's grace is his name not found among their number.

Prisoner Relations

Unlike the stories of friendship, support, and camaraderie that have come from other prison settings, there were no similar tales to tell from Jake's camp experiences. The slave labourers in the camps at Espenhain and Böhlen spent very little time socializing with each other. In the eight months he was in these camps, Jake only had relationships with three or four people. There were several reasons for this lack of bonding between people who were in the same predicament.

First, the Germans ensured that people were moved around frequently, so that people could not bond and join together in a revolt. They moved people between units in the camps and even between nearby camps. If people couldn't build relationships, they couldn't build the trust needed to plan seditious actions against the Germans.

Second, as alluded to previously, people in the camps didn't usually last that long. While there are no readily available statistics as to what percentage of people survived these camps, according to Jake and other survivors of these camps, a large percentage didn't make it. At the larger camp of Buchenwald, the death rate approached 25 percent, and Jake suspects it was even higher in the smaller camps. After his first three months in Espenhain, Jake estimates that about one hundred out of the three hundred who came with him had already died. Another survivor of a BRABAG camp testified later that, of the thirteen hundred people who arrived with him at the camp, only three hundred survived the back-breaking work.

The third reason that the slave labourers didn't associate with each other much was that they spent every moment they weren't working trying to get some sleep. Given the long days and the heavy work they were required to complete, they returned to their barracks exhausted. In addition, they worked seven days a week, so they did not have any time off to recuperate. The prisoners also soon noticed that a lack of sleep was a very quick path to the mortuary. Those who didn't sleep simply died from exhaustion. Sleep was so important for Jake that, even when there were bombings, he rarely left his bed. He knew that without sleep he wasn't going to survive.

The final reason that the slave labourers never really bonded is that they didn't trust each other. The Germans would reward people who brought them information about the past or current "misdeeds" of the other prisoners. As a result, there was always someone who would be ready to turn you in if you shared too much or you said the wrong thing. This was a common occurrence in German concentration camps. In the following section from his book, *Survival in Auschwitz*, Primo Levi tells how prisoners would betray each other:

> He (Schepschel) did not hesitate to have Moischl, his accomplice in a theft from the kitchen, condemned to a flogging in the mistaken hope of gaining favour in the eyes of the Blockaltester and furthering his candidature for the position of Kesselwascher, "vat-washer."[xxvii]

Viktor Frankl also speaks of the self-preservationist attitude that existed in his book *Man's Search for Meaning*:

> On average, only those prisoners could keep alive who, after years of trekking from camp to camp, had lost all scruples in their fight for existence; they were prepared to use every means, honest and otherwise, even brutal force, theft, and betrayal of their friends, in order to save themselves.[xxviii]

The mistrust was intensified due to the theft that occurred in the camp. People would use whatever means necessary to survive, even if it meant depriving another prisoner of their meager rations. As Jake put it, "Even if you prayed and closed your eyes your food was gone." The prevalence of theft was not unique to the camps where Jake was imprisoned. Primo Levi talked about the issue of theft in Auschwitz as well:

> We have learnt, on the other hand, that everything can be stolen and is in fact automatically stolen as soon as attention is relaxed.[xxix]

The Things People Will Do for Food

The lack of food was the biggest issue that faced the slave labourers in the company camps. It was simple: if a prisoner relied solely on the food provided by the camp administration, he would die. Those who were determined to survive found ways to supplement the food they received. Jake was no exception in this, and he came up with a number of ways to get extra rations.

The first thing that Jake did was trade his watch to the company foreman for additional bread. He also traded the wallet that his dad had given to his brother Neil as a gift. He felt bad about this, as he understood the emotional significance that the wallet held for Neil, especially since their father had passed away. But he had no choice. Without the extra food, he would die too. Unfortunately, Jake quickly ran out of things to trade. The only possessions he had left were his engagement ring and his Bible; both items he could not bring himself to trade.

One day when Jake was working outside he saw some big heaps of soil. Based on his knowledge of farming, he thought that there must be potatoes under those piles. To keep potatoes fresh, the farmers would put the potatoes in a hole in the soil. They would cover the potatoes with straw to ensure they wouldn't freeze. Finally they would cover the straw with soil to protect everything from the elements.

So at night Jake went out of the camp for about five kilometres and stole some of those potatoes. As it was colder in Germany than in the Netherlands, they buried the potatoes deeper in the ground. In the Netherlands they were typically under six inches of soil. In this part of Germany the potatoes were over eighteen inches down. Jake had to reach far down into the hole to get the potatoes and eventually had to use a stick just to reach them.

As most prisoners in the camp worked in the mine, they would bring back some coal in their pockets to heat the barracks. The group would put the coal in a little stove they had, and then use the heat to cook the potatoes. While

Jake ensured he had enough to eat for himself, he also shared what he could with the other prisoners.

Jake, along with two other men he felt he could trust, would go to the piles twice a week to steal potatoes. Their mission was very dangerous, because the potatoes were closely guarded. At night the three men would not return with the bus but would wait until it was very dark. They would then sneak through the guards and take as many potatoes as they could carry. They had to walk a few hours to get back to camp. That was also dangerous, because guards had patrols everywhere. When they got back, they could not use the regular entrance because the guards checked everyone there. So they snuck through a side entrance instead. They would have been punished severely if they had been caught with stolen food.

As it got colder, the group continued to help themselves to the potatoes. Since there were fewer patrols in the cold weather, it was somewhat easier. There was a long cold spell of at least twenty-five degrees, with a lot of snow. They kept taking potatoes from the same place, and they stuffed the empty space with straw. When the cold snap was finished, Jake didn't dare to go anymore. He was worried that the pit would collapse as the ground began to thaw. They had removed so many potatoes that there wasn't much left to hold up the soil. Sure enough, the pit did collapse with the warming weather. The Nazi guards were now aware of what had happened. Several prisoners who foolishly did try to take potatoes again were apprehended and shot.

Jake's luck was to run out as well. When he was cooking one of the last batches of potatoes, the guards stormed in and demanded to know where they had came from. Apparently they had been tipped off by one of the other inmates. Fortunately for Jake, they were only concerned with the potatoes he had with him at the time and didn't know about the potatoes he'd stolen previously.

The guards took Jake and one of his friends away to interrogate them. Because Jake's friend kept denying any involvement, he was beaten to within an inch of his life. Jake thought he'd better take a different approach if he was to save himself some serious pain. So when they asked him how he had got the potatoes, he came up with a good but completely false explanation. He said that he had obtained some soap, and he had traded with another camp member for the potatoes. He claimed to have no idea where the potatoes came from before that. When they asked him who this contact was, Jake said he hadn't asked his name. The Germans then asked him if he could identify the culprit if he saw him. Jake said he could do that, so they posted him at the gate of the factory to see if he could spot the perpetrator. Jake "looked very hard" but naturally never found the guilty party. Seeing that they were getting nowhere, the guards eventually dropped the matter.

As the war wore on and it became clear that the Germans were losing their advantage, more and more resources were called to the front. Soon there were not enough guards to track who went to work and who did not. As a result, many people stopped going to work altogether. But the guards came up with a new system to counter the newfound "laziness" in the labourers. Coupons were issued at work, which the prisoners had to hand in at night. If prisoners didn't have a card, they were punished and received no food. That didn't last long, because after a particular heavy bombing, the coupons were scattered everywhere and everyone could find as many coupons as they needed. Once this was discovered by the Germans, they introduced a date stamp for the coupons.

As a result of the date stamp system, everyone was forced back to work. But Jake had just gotten used to the idea of not working, so the thought of going back really bothered him. After digging around in the rubble, he eventually found one of the date stamps. He could now stamp the right dates on his collection of coupons. This trickery was not discovered, and Jake didn't have to work for the final month he was at the camp. He actually managed to save that stamp and took it back home with him. Regrettably, the stamp has been lost sometime in the last sixty-five years.

While he had the stamp, Jake could continue to get the daily rations that were due to those who had worked. Unfortunately, as the war progressed, these daily rations continued to shrink. Even though he wasn't working, Jake still needed more food to survive. Things began to get very bad, and many people were dying.

As Jake wasn't working, he tried to use his free time during the day to find food. He decided to set out with his friend John to find some work on a local farm. They were forced by necessity, since they were down to eating some sugar beets that he had found on the road, food that was usually reserved for animals. Jake thought that if they could find some additional employment they could either make some money and buy food, or simply receive food in lieu of wages.

Jake and John decided to first try a farm about five kilometres away. They would start out on the road that went from the factory to the mines in order to avoid suspicion, since what they were doing was strictly forbidden. Once they were far enough away, they would change directions and head over to the rural farming areas. Jake and John went to different farmers and told them that the two of them were on night duty, but that they were so hungry that they were willing to work during the day in return for some food. But the one farmer didn't dare, another had no work, and another simply didn't want to help. On the two of them went, but without any luck.

Later that day they came to a rather large farm. A Russian girl was outside shoveling manure. When Jake asked about work, she suggested that they talk to the foreman who was milking in the barn. So they proceeded into the barn in order to speak with the man. He became so angry that he grabbed a stick and, ranting and raving, tried to assault them. Jake and John ran away as fast as they could.

That episode gave them both quite a scare, and John, who was a little more timid, wanted to give up and go back. But there was one farm they hadn't visited, and Jake convinced him to try that last one. Jake opened the gate and went inside, while John followed hesitantly, holding open the gate in case they had to beat a hasty retreat. Going up to the door, Jake called to see if anyone was there. After a little while, a woman appeared. He told her their story and after looking them over, the woman asked them to wait while she got the foreman. They waited rather uneasily, as the last episode with a foreman was still fresh in their minds. As the gate had swung shut, John went back to prop it open, just to be on the safe side.

After waiting a while longer, it appeared that nothing was happening, so they decided to go. The lady noticed them leaving and asked them to wait just a little while longer. Finally the foreman came to the door; he was a fat man of about sixty. Unlike the last foreman they had encountered, this man had a friendly expression on his face. He inquired if Jake and John could do field work, and they quickly replied that they could. John, overcoming his timid nature, raised his skinny arm and pointed to where he used to have some muscles, indicating that he was a willing worker.

The two men started work right away, filling in bomb craters in the field. There had been heavy bombing recently, and there were approximately eighty craters scattered across the field. The foreman got them shovels, and the woman who lived at the farm brought them six large sandwiches, each with a thick layer of bacon grease. They were ecstatic about the prospect of eating real food and ate the sandwiches immediately. The foreman then showed them where to start work and left them there.

After a few hours, a French prisoner joined them. He had steady work at the farm. They had a lively discussion in German. It turned out that he had been here for five years and had found this farmer to be better than the others. While they were talking, the air raid siren went off, giving everyone quite a shock. There was no immediate danger, but they still felt better getting away from open ground.

Not too far away, on a hill nearby, was a small extermination camp. In this camp even the strongest men died in a few weeks. Jake and John had to go right by there in order to reach an air raid shelter, but the area was strictly off-limits without a pass. Unfortunately, neither of them had such a pass. Since the allied forces had already dropped so many bombs in the field, they decided to risk it. There was nobody checking papers at the entrance, so they managed to get into the shelter unnoticed. But they were far from feeling at ease. They tried to be inconspicuous by sitting in a dark corner, but the presence of the SS men in the bunker worried them a lot. Finally, the sirens stopped, and they left as quickly as possible. Soon they arrived safely back on the road. They were relieved to be safe and decided that they would never take such a risk again.

Meanwhile, back at the farm it was lunch time. Because of the alarm, the food wasn't quite ready yet, so Jake and John had to work in the barn for a while. There was a container of cooked potatoes meant for the pigs, and the hungry men helped themselves to some of that food. Finally it was lunchtime. First they were served soup, then potatoes with hamburger, and finally four pancakes. They just couldn't believe their good fortune. They could not recall ever having eaten a meal that tasted so good. After surviving so long on terrible-tasting food that provided almost no nourishment, they were overwhelmed by the experience of eating a real meal.

After they had finished, the farmer's wife gave them each four of the same large sandwiches along for coffee time. They were flabbergasted. For almost a year they had been used to working long days, with only one small meal to tide them over, and now suddenly they had several good meals in one day. But they still felt incredibly hungry and devoured the sandwiches immediately.

The other men at the farm worked until 6:30, but Jake and John had to be back at the barracks by 6:00. Since the people on the farm thought that Jake and John had to go on night shift, they were allowed to leave early. While they were putting away their shovels and other tools, the kind woman called them over. She gave them each a bowl of soup, which they gratefully ate. As they were leaving, she handed them a lunch to take along and also gave them twenty kilograms of raw potatoes, which they could cook themselves. They had not been so happy in a very long time. They ate the sandwiches on the way home because, once again, they just couldn't wait any longer.

When Jake and John got back to camp, the other prisoners were naturally very surprised at their good fortune. They immediately cooked the potatoes and shared them with the others. They felt that since they would be going back to that farm again, they could afford to be generous. The next morning they got up at 3:30, happy to return to the farm. They wanted to put in a full day's work, as requested by the foreman.

They had gone a ways down the road when they met a group of Russian prisoners who were also going to work. That was quite normal, but a while later they met another group of people. It was still dark, so at first they couldn't see who the strangers were. Once they found out they got the scare of their lives. The strangers were members of the wheelbarrow brigades from the nearby extermination camp. There were prisoners of every nationality—Russians, Poles, Belgians, Dutchmen, etc.—and their guards were terribly vicious.

They were almost past the group when one of the guards stopped Jake and John and demanded to see their identification. Unfortunately, the papers Jake and John possessed did not allow them to be in that area, and consequently they were in trouble. After being questioned by the guards, they received a thorough beating. The others in the group had stopped further down the road, and Jake and John were told to join them. In desperation, John suggested that they should make a break for it. Jake refused, as he saw the guards had drawn their revolvers. There was nothing else they could do but go along with the crowd.

When the group came to the camp, the guards first administered another round of beatings before putting Jake and John to work. They had to load trucks with a chemical used to create a smokescreen around factories when there was an air raid. It was extremely poisonous. Jake doesn't know exactly what chemicals they were working with, but to this day he suspects that the large number of marks and moles he has on his back are related to the exposure he had to these toxic materials.

Everyone shoveled madly, because the German guards would lash out at the slightest provocation. It was cold and raining, but Jake and John were not allowed to put on their coats. Four men shoveled the chemicals into a pile, and then two more had to shovel it onto a wagon. After working for only a little while, they were already utterly exhausted, but they had no choice but to continue. Fortunately, there was an air raid, which gave them a welcome rest. Then and there they agreed that, if they got away from this camp, they would never go to work for a farmer again.

Eventually the camp commander sent them back to their own camp with a letter for their local commander. As Jake could read a little German, he opened the envelope and read the contents. To his surprise, the letter instructed the commander of his local camp to execute him. Jake was carrying his own death warrant. He immediately decided that he would never show the letter to his camp commander. For a while he thought that he might keep the letter as a really interesting souvenir. He thought twice when he realized the high possibility of getting captured by anther German commander and having his letter discovered. So he burned the letter instead.

While Jake and John had agreed that they would never go back to work on the farm, their resolve lasted for all of one evening. The food beckoned them so strongly that the very next morning they set out for the farm again. While they were cautious on their journey, they reached the farm without incident. When they arrived, they received more food and then went right to work. They returned to work at the farm for the next few weeks.

For all the things Jake was willing to do to get food, there were a few things he just wouldn't do. First, he wouldn't eat any spoiled or rotten food. While others grew so desperate they would eat anything, Jake rightly believed that the likelihood of getting ill did not justify the risk. One time Jake saw the guards spill a whole container of soup outside of the barracks. Some of the prisoners were so famished that they went and scooped up the spilled soup even though it was on the same ground where the prisoners relieved themselves in the evenings. Jake also refused to beg outside of the camp, even though many others did. He felt that in order to survive, he had to maintain some level of dignity. And finally, Jake never reduced himself to stealing food from other inmates. As mentioned earlier, this was such a common practice that if you had food and closed your eyes to ask God for a blessing, the food would be gone. Given what the Germans did to him, he had no problem taking things from them, as a sort of "payment for services rendered." But he could never bring himself to justify stealing from another fellow prisoner just so he could survive.

The Bombing of the Böhlen Factory

By mid-1944 the tide of the war had clearly shifted. The Allied forces went from being on the defensive to being the aggressors. They gained air superiority over the depleted German air force and began long-range bombing runs deep into German territory. Their most important targets were the fuel production facilities, which they bombed continuously for almost a year.

The Germans were not ones to give up easily, so they installed huge batteries of anti-aircraft guns. These sophisticated guns worked together in groups of twelve to target individual planes. They would fire together from multiple angles to ensure that their target was brought down. These giant guns fired 88-mm shells, and Jake still remembers how the earth would shake when the guns at Espenhain and Böhlen went off.

If the Allied bombers made it past the guns, they would then have to deal with waves of German fighter planes. The English and Americans countered by sending more planes than the Germans could shoot down. Often they would send two or three hundred bombers at once to attack the factory at Böhlen. While they generally succeeded at doing some damage to the factory, the Germans would use the slave labour resources they had at their disposal to fix the damage and carry on operations.

From May 1944 until March 1945, the Allied forces dropped a total of 11,280 bombs on the factory at Böhlen with a combined weight of 2.5 million pounds. The following details are based on British Royal Air Force bombing records:[xxx]

- May 12, 1944—1,030 bombs
- June 29, 1944—1,600 bombs
- August 16, 1944—1,000 bombs
- September 11, 1944—500 bombs
- September 12, 1944—500 bombs
- October 7, 1944—1,500 bombs
- November 30, 1944—500 bombs
- February 13, 1945—700 bombs
- February 17, 1945—1,500 bombs
- February 20, 1945—250 bombs
- March 2, 1945—100 bombs
- March 17, 1945—100 bombs
- March 21, 1945—2,000 bombs

Jake was in Böhlen for the bombings that occurred in 1945. There were also several bombings in Espenhain, but they did not reach the same level as Böhlen. Records indicate that about three thousand bombs were dropped on the factory complex in Espenhain over the same period of time.

Jake described one of these air raids as follows:

One morning the air raid sirens went again. Since this happened frequently, we didn't pay much attention. We were not allowed to leave anyways but had to continue our work. On previous occasions, we seldom even saw an airplane, but this time it was different. Formation after formation flew directly over the gun installation. The Germans were shooting furiously at them. It was a terrible noise. There were twenty-four anti-aircraft guns that fired simultaneously at one airplane. Of the approximately one thousand airplanes that passed overhead, the Germans shot down about five. We weren't working, of course, because shrapnel was flying all over the place. We just sort of huddled together until it was finished.

One of the bombings in Espenhain was so severe that, when it was finished, Jake saw train cars that had been deposited on the roofs of factories. He himself would not have believed such a thing was possible unless he had seen it with his own eyes. When he got back after the war, many of his friends didn't believe his story either. They thought he was stretching the truth a little. Fortunately for Jake, he managed to locate a photo of that very scene and was able to prove to them that his story was not a fabrication.

Since the camps where the slave labourers lived were small and closely connected to the factories, they were as much at risk of being hit by bombs as any other building. Unlike the concentration camps near major cities that the Allied forces purposely avoided bombing, in Espenhain and Böhlen the camps got hit as well.

Even though the air force pilots were endangering Jake's life by dropping their bombs, Jake never felt any resentment against them. Rather, he admired the courage that allowed them to fly directly into enemy fire without wavering. They would continue forward until either the job was done or they were shot down. Jake also imagined these young men in their tight quarters in the airplane, and he empathized with their situation. Every time an American Flying Fortress or British Lancaster bomber was shot down, fourteen young men would go with it. And yet they continued to fly directly into the path of those anti-aircraft guns in order to complete their missions.

The two most historically significant bombings took place on February 13 and March 21 of 1945. The February bombing was part of a larger operation called Operation Thunderclap. This Operation was the very controversial firebombing of Dresden in which over fifty thousand German civilians lost their lives. During this operation, the factory at Böhlen was used as a decoy to take German focus away from the true target of Dresden. Fortunately for the Germans, during this attack there was heavy cloud cover at Böhlen and the attack did little real damage.[xxxi]

The story was quite different on March 21. This time the target was solely the factory at Böhlen, and the Allied forces were determined to deliver a knockout punch. It was a clear day, and they dropped more bombs than they had ever dropped in the past. The factory was obliterated and was still in ruins when the Allied tanks rolled into to the facility on April 19, 1945.

Germans Only Please

The bombing on March 21 was unlike anything Jake had experienced before. The camp was being pounded. The earth was shaking, and there were explosions everywhere. Even from below Jake could tell the Allied planes hadn't come to just drop a few bombs. They were definitely there to destroy the factory once and for all. Jake says that the sight of over one thousand planes in the air is difficult to describe. When they flew over, there were so many of them that the sky would darken. Their engines gave off so much condensation that they appeared to be flying in a fog. The sound of the engines and propellers was only drowned out by the sound of bombs exploding on the ground and in the factory.

As Jake was now in Böhlen and there was a bomb shelter, he decided that this particular attack was so severe that it would be wise to seek refuge. He ran across camp and asked the guards to let him into the bomb shelter. They drove him off at gunpoint, saying that the shelter was for Germans only; no Dutch people were allowed.

So Jake went to look for shelter elsewhere. Eventually he decided to hide out in the mine. This option was not really that safe, as if a bomb fell anywhere near a mine shaft entrance, the entrance would collapse and the people in the mine would be trapped. But to Jake it still seemed to be a better option than staying out in the open. He hid in the cold, dark, wet mine shaft waiting for bombing to end. It was one of the most frightening experiences of his life. He couldn't see what was happening, but he could hear all the loud explosions, and he could feel the ground shake beneath him. He was petrified that, at any moment, one of those bombs would fall in the opening to his mine shaft and would bury him forever. That bombing lasted for an incredible eight hours, during which time many of the factory buildings were destroyed or severely damaged.

When Jake came out of the mine, he was shocked to see that the bomb bunker had been destroyed. This bunker had been built to survive many attacks and had the reputation among the Germans of being indestructible. If all the bombs had fallen on the outside of the bunker, the Germans would have probably been right. But in this case, a bomb fell through the air intake of the bomb shelter and exploded inside. The contained space and thick walls ensured that most of the force of the blast was contained within the bunker, killing everyone instantly. By driving Jake away, the Germans had in fact saved his life. If they had let him in, he would have perished with the rest of them.

How Low Can You Get?

It was during his time in the factory camps that Jake experienced his most difficult moments. He never broke completely, but there were times of suffering and despair that brought Jake lower than he'd ever been. Without the strength of his faith, he would have rolled over and died, like many of the others around him.

As was common with most of the inmates, Jake ended up getting sick. But when Jake fell ill, it was so bad that it almost killed him. He had been working on the anti-aircraft guns out in the cold of winter when there had been an air raid. Jake and some of the other prisoners were huddled together trying to avoid the bombs and the flying shrapnel. That attack lasted an hour. Once it was over, they had to go back to work. While they were working, Jake started to feel quite sick. Then as the prisoners walked for thirty minutes to get to their bus, he began to experience excruciating cramps and diarrhea. By the time they got back to the camp, he as shivering so badly he could barely stand. He went straight to bed and barely had the strength to get himself up onto his bunk (they had moved the barracks by this time, and bunks had replaced the bags of straw on the floor). That night the bunks were moving so much from his shivering that the people below him couldn't sleep.

So there Jake was, lying in bed almost too sick to move. But the Germans weren't going to let him lie in bed all day and recover. He either had to be declared unfit to work before his shift was to begin or he had to tough it out and go to work. If the guards came to get someone for their shift and the prisoner said he was too sick to go, the guards considered it an act of rebellion for which the prisoner would be punished. At 4:30 in the morning, Jake had to get himself out of bed and go to the camp medical officer, known as the "Sanitater," to get himself declared unfit to work.

Jake trudged though camp in the darkness to see the Sanitater. Unfortunately for him, the camp commander was also at the Sanitater's office at the time and he had an intense dislike for Dutchmen. He wanted to throw Jake out immediately and send him back to work. Fortunately, Jake knew some German and was able to convince the commander of his need for treatment. Eventually he was able to see the Sanitater. Things didn't get much better, as the Sanitater wanted to give him a pill and send him back to work. Jake knew that if he went to work that day he probably wouldn't come back. He pushed for the Sanitater to take his temperature. While the man got angry, he eventually agreed to do so. Jake was running an extremely high temperature of forty-one degrees, enough that camp rules said he was unfit to work (if you had a temperature of thirty-nine degrees, you still had to work). Reluctantly, the Sanitater and the camp commander decided he should report to the sick bay.

Off Jake trudged again through the cold, rainy night to the sick bay, which was located all the way across camp. When he got there, things didn't get any easier for him. The person who operated the sick bay didn't want to admit him and said they only took new patients at night. By this time Jake had learned to be insistent and showed a letter he had from the camp commander saying he was unfit to work. The sick bay operator now knew he would have to let Jake in, but he was still determined to make it hard for Jake. So he said that, before Jake could come in, he had to get himself and his clothes disinfected.

Jake dragged his half-dead body the 1.5 kilometres to the disinfection centre, where the people who ran the facility promptly told him that they only disinfected groups of thirty people or more. Perhaps it was how ill Jake really appeared or maybe it was the murderous look in his eyes that eventually convinced them to do the disinfection. His clothes went in an oven to kill all the bugs, and Jake had to stand in the shower for thirty minutes. Normally this was a warm shower, but since the boilers hadn't been started, he had to stand for thirty minutes under cold water, making his condition even worse. He finally got his disinfection papers and trudged back to the sick bay where he was shown to his room. It was now 11:00. The camp administration had made a man who was near death march back and forth across camp for six hours.

The ironic part of the situation was that once Jake actually got into the sick bay, he received absolutely no treatment. The only thing the staff did was check to make sure he was still alive. Their sole function was to remove the dead bodies. So Jake laid there for four days drifting in and out of consciousness. He is sure that he slipped into a coma for a few of those days, but since there was no medical staff looking after him, he can't be positive. After the four days were up, the staff came and ordered him back to work, ignoring the fact that he was still deathly ill. Somehow he managed to get up and go back to work, and eventually he started to get better.

While the physical illness nearly killed him, it was the emotional strain that was even harder to bear. Until he had been arrested, Jake had led a very sheltered, protected life. He had come from a small community where everyone knew each other and had always had his family close by. And now here he was, hundreds of kilometres from home, being worked to death with no end in sight. He had no friends or family to talk to, people dying all around him, and little hope of seeing his family again. For a "simple" country boy, it was almost too much to bear. The sadness and loneliness were overwhelming.

Making matters even worse was the fact that it was very dangerous to express your emotions in the camp. With the Nazi guards, the more you cried, the harder they punished. Apparently it was satisfying for them because their actions had the desired result. Jake found that even if he had a lot of pain, it was better not to show it. He never gave them the satisfaction of knowing how their treatment was affecting him. In the long run his approach paid off, as the guards tended to leave him alone. However, in the short term being able to cry would have brought great relief and having to remain stoic made the emotional suffering even harder to bear.

Being worked nearly to death for months, without receiving nearly enough food, was taking its toll on Jake. As he put it, "What hunger does is it takes the will out of you, even the will to live. All you wanted to do was lie down and give up." Even though he did what he could to get extra food, there was never enough.

As many starving people around the world can attest, the feeling of intense hunger is extremely painful and completely unlike the hunger that the rest of us may feel in our lives. Jake describes this hunger in the following way:

> There are things that you cannot describe. You can think of it. Before I was there I would say "Mom, I'm hungry, can I have something to eat?" Well that is not hunger. Real hunger you cannot describe. It's an awful feeling that you can get only when you just about die from hunger.

In *Man's Search for Meaning*, Viktor Frankl describes this hunger in an even deeper way:

> Those who have not gone through a similar experience can hardly conceive of the soul destroying mental conflict and clashes of will power which a famished man experiences.[xxxii]

Perhaps the most visceral description of what this type of hunger is really like comes from another Dutchman who survived the Nazi labour camp system. In the book *Slave Labor*, author Joel Berman captures the feelings of prisoner Adrian Van De Ree in the following way:

I am so I hungry, I would eat bread covered with mud or dog shit, just flick off the fecal stains and put it into my mouth for whatever sustenance it gives. You think that behavior sick or stupid? You have not been truly hungry![xxxiii]

The prisoners soon learned that the time to really be afraid was when the hunger pain stopped. If they stopped feeling hungry, it meant that their bodies were shutting down and they couldn't eat anymore, even if they wanted to. If the pain stopped, they were as good as dead. So the prisoners lived each day with the awful combination of suffering through the pain but also praying that it wouldn't stop.

The conditions the prisoners were held in made matters much worse for Jake. The fact that they were treated worse than animals was so humiliating and dehumanizing that he could scarcely bear it. They could never wash, so they started to smell in the worst way. Prisoners smelled so bad that they would vomit because of their own stench. And half of the camp had dysentery. But there were not nearly enough bathrooms, so people soiled themselves without getting cleaned up. There would be lineups of seventy men for a single bathroom, with most unable to wait until it was their turn. There was no toilet paper and not nearly adequate washing facilities. As a result of the unsanitary conditions, the camps were full of disease.

To this day Jake struggles to describe just how bad things actually were at the camp. He simply can't find the words to describe the conditions he witnessed.

But feelings are very hard to convey in words, and one person is better than another. You may say I talk a lot, but I wish I was better at describing the feelings. I have been in transport where there is only room for you to lay on the floor. And half of the prisoners have contagious dysentery with one bathroom. Imagine that you have one bathroom and there are seventy people in front of you and you really, really have to go with diarrhea. How do you feel? Can you describe that? And if you step over the people? And if you shit over the people? That's what was happening. How do you describe that?

Jake is not alone in these struggles. In the introduction to his book *Night*, Nobel Prize winning author Elie Wiesel talks about his challenge is describing his experiences in Auschwitz and Buchenwald:

Convinced that the period in history would be judged on day, I knew that I must bear witness. I also knew that, while I had many things to say, I did not have the words to say them . . .. Hunger—thirst—fear—transport—selection—fire—chimney: these words all have intrinsic meaning but, in those times, they meant something else.[xxxiv]

In his time at the factory camps, Jake believes he hit the bottom; that he could not possibly experience any more suffering than he had, that he could not get any lower. He believes that this limit is different for everyone, but that at some point, you simply don't feel any more pain. He describes the experience as follows:

It's hard to explain, but I cannot say what was the deepest of the feeling. It slowly got worse. Every time it was worse you would have a setback. In the beginning you had hope they would get you out, but after a while you don't have that hope anymore. When you lose that, that is a big thing. I think you come to a point where there is no lower; there is a bottom. Even if it gets worse you are at the bottom already. Even if it gets worse, you cannot get lower. I don't know where my bottom is, but I feel like I reached that point. If you really hurt, you can try to hurt yourself more, but you don't feel it because it hurts less than what you already have. You're in as much pain as you can feel. Your body shuts off because you are at the limit and the limit is different for everyone.

There are large periods of time at the camp of which Jake has no recollection. This gap isn't a result of his age today; he couldn't remember them even when he had just returned home. What he does know is that he went through a gradual process where his conscious mind started to shut off. He would robotically go through the motions, but he wasn't consciously aware of what was happening. He believes that this was his body's defense mechanism trying to keep him alive, as there were times that he didn't feel like he could go on any further.

Through all his suffering, it was Jake's faith that sustained him and kept him from fearing his captors. He would often think of Job, who cried out to the Lord during his suffering, or of the Psalms when David would cry out for the Lord's help. God would provide him the strength he needed to make it through another day. The following is Jake's description of the role his faith played in his survival:

All at once everything is completely ripped apart. Then the Lord is like an anchor. There is really no other place to go for help. Where else could you go? So then you go and read Psalms and other pieces of the Bible and you're comforted. Even when you are in deep despair, there is always something uplifting. I cannot go into too much detail as a lot of it was in my mind. It's not always that you can go to concrete things, but it's a feeling of closeness. You feel that someone is watching you. You are asked to do things that you think you could never do, and you feel that you are at the end. But God gives you that little more strength you need to still survive another day.

Jacob Van Seters and Agnieta (Iet) Korsten in 1946.

Jacob and Agnieta (Iet) Van Seters with their children in the 1950s.

Jacob and Elma Van Seters in 2009.

Jake parasailing in Mexico in 2009 (at the age of eighty-six).

Kamp Vught in 1945.

Kamp Vught today.

The police station in Haagseveer, Rotterdam, as it appeared in 1944.

The still operational police station in Haagseveer today.

A war memorial within the Haagseveer police station.

A prison notification regarding the amount of correspondence Jake was allowed to send.

Kamp Amersfoort as it appeared in the 1940s.

Kamp Amersfoort today.

"The Stone Man" statue at Kamp Amersfoort, in the shooting range.

An original guard tower at Kamp Amersfoort.

The actory complex in Espenhain as it would have looked in the 1940s.

One of the few remaining buildings from the Epsenhain factory complex.

The factory complex in Böhlen as it would have appeared in the 1940s.

The Böhlen factory being bombed by the RAF on March 21, 1945.

The Lippendorf Power plant that sits in place of the old Böhlen factory.

The Dow Chemical plant also built on the Böhlen factory property.

A mass grave of workers from the Troeglitz labour camp, located thirty kilometres from Böhlen.

A memorial to the Dutch prisoners in the camp at Böhlen.

Plaques with the names of the Dutch prisoners who died at Böhlen.

The Van Seters' family crest.

Chapter 6: The Escape

By the beginning of April 1945, the fighting was getting closer and closer to Böhlen. The Americans had been pushing the Germans back from the south, and the front was rapidly approaching the factory. The bombing raids occurred with increased frequency, and there were airplanes in the sky constantly. The ground shook all day from the battle going on around the camp.

Time to Get out of Dodge

As Jake was returning to the camp one evening, he heard a new type of warning alarm going off. While normally the air raid warning would go off, this time the alarm sounded for a tank attack. Jake then saw some of the German soldiers retreating in a badly damaged car, while others were changing into civilian clothes to avoid being captured. The fighting around the camp had become very intense, with bullets flying everywhere. Thinking that the Americans must have broken through, Jake returned to camp to get some of his belongings. But when he got there, he found the camp surrounded by German soldiers who were loading up the remaining prisoners to move them deeper into Germany. As the last thing Jake wanted was to be sent further into Germany, he and some of the other prisoners made a dash for the mine. They hid there all night, thinking that by morning they would be liberated.

The next morning when they woke up, the shooting had stopped. Thinking they were now free, they headed back to camp to get their things. Their intention was to follow up their return to the camp with a visit to the farmer who had helped them. After saying good-bye one last time, they would be on their way home. Unfortunately, their joy was short lived that morning as they were apprehended by German soldiers almost immediately after leaving the mine. They were led away with a large number of prisoners who were being transferred to other camps.

Jake and his fellow prisoners walked for five kilometres to the train station where their transport was waiting. As they were walking, there was another air raid. During the confusion, they managed to escape again and tried to leave by another route. But like the first time, they were quickly recaptured.

They escaped a total of three times, only to be recaptured each time. One time they made it to the forest and hid there overnight. In the end, they got too hungry and had to come out again. Fortunately, the Germans were in such a state of disarray that they were no longer executing people who were caught trying to escape. They just rounded them up and put them on the trains. Only a few months earlier they would have been killed for their actions. In the book *Slave Labor*, Joel Berman tells several different stories of prisoners who attempted to escape and were executed as a result.[xxxv]

After being captured a final time, Jake was forced to march again, this time for thirty kilometres, with no food. The prisoners' feet were raw and bleeding, but still they had to press on. When he couldn't take it anymore, Jake escaped, along with a group of four other men. This time they weren't caught. They headed off into the countryside, attempting to find their way to freedom.

While Jake never found out where the prisoners were being sent, it's probably a very good thing he escaped when he did. If he had been sent to the camps in the city of Leipzig, some twenty kilometres north of Böhlen, he might never have made it home. On April 18, 1945, the Nazis massacred 250 slave labourers in a camp near Leipzig. They herded the victims into a building and set off a bomb. The building subsequently burst into flames, and many of those not killed in the blast were burned alive. The few who managed to break down the doors to get out were mowed down by machine gun fire from the Nazi guards. Thirty kilometres to the south west, at the BRABAG work camp at Troeglitz, things were just as bad. Four hundred prisoners were executed and buried in a mass grave, just days before the Allied forces arrived.[xxxvi]

Life in No-man's Land

Once they were free, Jake and his fellow prisoners found themselves with a new problem. They were behind enemy lines. If they were to get to freedom, they would have to find some way to get to the other side. The German front was to the south of them, while the American front was beyond that. Each side had rows of artillery, tanks, and infantry. First, both sides would fire the artillery at each other. Then, as they got closer, they would send the tanks in to fight. Finally, when they were almost on top of each other, the infantry would take over.

Not seeing any other options, the group decided to cross the battlefield. They managed to sneak through the German lines during the night and hide in a haystack. Before they could make a break for the American lines, the fighting broke out again in earnest. They stayed in that haystack for three days, without food and water, as the conflict raged around them. Finally, it became too dangerous for them to stay in the haystack, due to the stray bullets and shrapnel from both sides. During a lull in the fighting, they made a break for a nearby farm, where a kind German farmer allowed them to hide in his barn. That night the fighting intensified even more. All they heard was the constant sound of gunfire, and bullets even began whizzing though the barn. The men scrambled to build a barricade of large stones in the barn. The battle continued all night, and Jake regularly heard the ping of bullets ricocheting off their hastily-assembled barricade. When they looked outside, they saw the whole sky illuminated with spotlights and tracer fire. It was a terrifying, yet awe-inspiring sight.

By morning all was quiet. Because it had been a brutally cold night, they decided to build themselves a fire to warm themselves by. Just as they got it going, the farmer, who had been hiding in the house all night, burst into the barn. "The Americans are here!" he shouted. And sure enough, when they got outside, they saw the huge American tanks rumbling toward them. It appeared that the Germans had fled late at night, and now the Americans were on their way to track down their enemies.

The group watched as the tanks tore through the nearby town. They churned up the roads with their big tracks. When they were too wide to fit down the narrow village streets, they simply knocked the houses over as if they were made of matchsticks. The German residents were quick to hang white flags out of their windows as a sign of surrender. Soon the town was a sea of white.

At first the abrupt change in their situation was a little much for them to comprehend. But they soon snapped out of their trance and started yelling in celebration. Finally they were free! They had waited for this moment for so long that it was hard for them to accept that it was really happening. They turned and hugged each other, tears streaming down their faces.

Meanwhile, some of the Americans had stopped their tanks in the shade of the nearby trees, so that their vehicles were out of sight of any remaining German aircraft. They emerged from the tanks with their guns drawn. There were covered in dust, and the stress of the days of fighting could be seen on their faces. Some were still so nervous that they could barely light their cigarettes.

The ragged group of men approached the Americans carefully. They told the soldiers that they were Dutchmen and that they hadn't eaten in five days. The Americans quickly warmed to them, giving them some food, some cigarettes (an absolute necessity in those days), and a gun for protection. Jake immediate smoked one of the cigarettes, a Lucky Strike. Due to the combination of an empty stomach and not having had real tobacco in so long, that one cigarette almost knocked him clear off his feet. Once he regained his composure, the Americans showed his group how to use the gun. Then the soldiers began a house-by-house search looking for hiding German soldiers. The Dutch group offered to help, and together they searched the first house, a castle that was nearby. The Germans inside offered no resistance, and the group quickly confiscated all their supplies.

Between them the Dutchmen ended up with five sides of bacon, one hundred kilograms of sugar, forty packages of pudding, eggs, butter, and much more. After a year of nearly starving to death, they now had more food than they could eat. They started by making the pudding. Using fifteen litres of milk, they cooked up two pails full of pudding. They put lots of sugar and eggs in the pudding, and even though it ended up being too sweet, they polished it off in record time. They were so full they couldn't move; they just laid down and reveled in the feeling of fullness. After being hungry for so long, being full was an absolutely wonderful experience. After a short time had passed, they felt hungry again, so they cooked up a large piece of pork and devoured that as well.

One Last Very Close Call

After taking some time to rest, the group of Dutchmen did what every group of young men in their twenties would do in such a situation; they went to the nearest pub for a celebratory beer. They were feeling great now and were in the mood to celebrate their freedom. They sat down and ordered beers for their entire group. They didn't actually have any money, but they knew the German bartender was not going to make a fuss if they didn't pay their bill.

No sooner had they received their beers than three German soldiers barged through the back door in full battle fatigues. One of them was clutching a grenade in his hand and was threatening to blow the place up. Jake and his fellow Dutchmen were terrified. They weren't just scared of the grenade. They were equally worried that the Americans outside the pub would see the German soldiers and come in with their guns blazing. After they got over their initial shock, they saw that one of the soldiers was very badly wounded. Half his face was missing, and he was bleeding everywhere. The other two German soldiers demanded that the bartender take care of their friend. If he refused, they threatened to blow up the whole bar. The bartender quickly agreed and took the wounded man off their hands. With that, the two other soldiers turned and headed out the back door as quickly as they had come in. The Dutchmen also left immediately after the incident, but in the opposite direction. The group was determined not to lose their newly found freedom. They reported the incident to the Americans, who dispatched some men to track down the German soldiers.

Not Quite Going Home

The next morning the group got up and after having a large and rather leisurely breakfast, they decided that they needed to clean themselves up. They washed themselves thoroughly with soap and water, a real luxury given their conditions of the previous year. The group then headed into town and split up for a while. Jake got a new set of clothes and more supplies. But he was outdone by one of the other men in the group who came back with a new bike that he had received from the Americans. The rest of the group decided that they also needed bikes so that they could all ride home to the Netherlands together. By this time the Americans had moved on in pursuit of the German army so the rest of the group had to find bikes through other means. After talking it over, they decided that they would ask the locals if they could have their bikes.

The Dutchmen had seen other groups of prisoners robbing and looting from the local Germans and even killing their families and animals. They were determined to remain courteous and civil and not stoop to the level of the German guards who had oppressed them. They also knew that the German civilians would probably give them the bikes out of fear anyway, but they agreed ahead of time that there would be no rough stuff. If their request was denied at a certain house, they would simply move on to the next one.

Within thirty minutes they all had nearly new bikes. Jake had a nice ladies' bike with balloon tires that rolled really well. Right away he began thinking about being back at home with Iet. So they decided that, once they had some more food, they would start heading home. By this time they had gotten in the habit of going to German houses and asking the people inside to prepare them a meal. Again, there was no rough treatment, but they felt it was the least they were owed. That morning they had breakfast at seven different houses before they left. Even though the fighting was still going on nearby, their need to get home was so strong that they decided to take the risk and started on their homeward journey that evening.

They were about seven hundred kilometres from the Netherlands' border at that time and thought that, even if they had a few setbacks, they could be home in fourteen days. They spent the rest of the day gathering supplies and were set to go by evening. Before they left, the farmer they had been staying with invited them in for dinner with him and his wife. They readily accepted, as this man had treated them well over the last number of days. He had not joined the Nazi party and yet had lost his son to the war. They ate their final meal and headed out.

Before heading for home, they decided to go back to the camp at Böhlen one last time. Jake really wanted to find his Bible. Along with his engagement ring, they were the only two possessions that he had managed to keep for the entire time he was way. The Bible had been a gift from Iet, and therefore had a lot of meaning for him. Plus, it had gotten him through many of the most difficult times of his imprisonment. While Böhlen wasn't all that far away, they men were not nearly in as good a shape as they thought, and the going was very slow. As they biked along, they saw the battle scars of the war all around them. There was debris everywhere, and there were dead Germans lying on the side of the road, still dressed in their combat uniforms. Entire towns and villages had been reduced to smoldering heaps of rubble.

When they got to the camp, they saw evidence of the fighting there as well. Many of the barracks were burned down, and everything was in a state of disarray. Even though his barrack had not been burned, Jake couldn't find his Bible in the debris. All he found was his shaving brush. Given the bad feelings they harbored toward the camp, the group decided that they should leave as soon as possible.

As Jake's group started heading toward the Netherlands, they noticed something happening that troubled them. The Americans had pulled back, and the Russians had been flooding into the area where they were riding. Before they had attacked Germany, the four main Allied countries (Britain, France, the United States, and Russia) had agreed on how they would carve up the conquered territory. The American forces had proceeded farther than that arrangement had specified and the Russian had requested that they return back to the agreed upon demarcation line. While the Americans had protested that they had the Germans on the run, the Russians had responded that they would get them eventually anyway. They wanted full credit for defeating the Germans, and they weren't about to let the Americans take that away from them.

The problem for Jake and his group was that the Russian army was far different than that of the Americans. As a result of years of seeing their families suffer and die because of the Germans, the Russians were bent on revenge. Many of the Russians were also poor peasant folk and were stealing everything they could get their hands on. If they saw a German with a nice watch they simply shot him and took it. They were killing Germans everywhere, stealing their possessions, and raping their women. While some of the anger the Russians felt may have been understandable given what their country had been through, it was terrifying to Jake and his group. In addition, there were rumors floating around that the Russians were deporting prisoners from the German concentration camps to their own prison camps (a rumor that, in many cases, turned out to be true). So the group rode as hard as they could and managed to stay just in front of the progressing Russian army. When they made it back into American-controlled territory, they breathed a collective sigh of relief.

For the next fourteen days they rode toward the Netherlands. They would stop occasionally to get food from the local Germans and then carry on with their journey. At night they would usually sleep at a farm, but occasionally they would also stop at inns or even in people's houses. Given their rough shape and the fact they were riding through mountainous terrain, they didn't make nearly the progress they had expected. By the fourteenth day they had only covered two hundred kilometres.

By now the group was getting impatient. They decided to start early the next day, in order to cover as much distance as they could. They started at 5:00 AM and were making some good progress. But that all changed a few hours later when they were stopped by an American soldier. To their annoyance and confusion, he confiscated their bikes and told them they were not allowed to continue. The Americans explained that there were too many fleeing prisoners on the road and that they needed to keep the roads clear to allow the army to move its equipment to and from the front lines. However, they promised to make arrangements to bring the group back to the Netherlands themselves. But Jake and his friends would just needed to be patient.

The Americans put them up in the local munitions factory, which had no beds and only sawdust on the floor. Jake's group didn't like that very much, so they soon found other accommodations. They found a nice room, which they furnished with three beds, a table, and three chairs. They also had a radio, an electric blanket, and a fan to keep things cool (it was starting to warm up by this time). Overall, it was quite comfortable. While they felt relaxed in their new surroundings, they still wanted to go home as soon as they could. But their departure kept getting delayed, so they ended up staying for five weeks.

The time they spent with the Americans actually turned out to be a blessing, as they were all in much worse shape than they realized. Their exuberance at being free had caused them to overlook how unhealthy their time in captivity had made them. All the men were infested with lice and scabies, and many of them were covered in boils. Even though they had washed, they were still dirty, and their clothes were still infested with bugs. The Americans had doctors with them and they took good care of the group. First the Americans cleaned and showered everyone properly, so the last remnants of the filth from the camps were washed away. Then they used DDT to kill all the lice and scabies; the former prisoners were now bug-free for the first time in a year. The time they spent with the Americans really helped the group to get healthy again and ensured that they would be properly presentable by the time they arrived home.

Jake had developed some very severe boils on his leg and on his neck. The boil on his leg burst when he hit his leg on a bar. This was actually a good thing, as it let the boil drain (they can't heal while full of puss). The one on his neck proved to be a much more difficult case. His years of slinging around heavy sacks of grain had caused his neck to become calloused, and the boil had formed under the callous. As such, it wouldn't burst. As it grew bigger, the doctors became concerned that if they left it the pus from the boil would enter his system and poison him. So the doctors had to cut it open to relieve the pressure. Jake still remembers with some amusement how, after the doctor had cut into the boil, puss and blood had sprayed over the attending nurse. Not surprisingly, she was somewhat less amused.

Having time on their hands, Jake and his group tried to find more supplies. One day Jake happened upon an American army barracks that had been recently abandoned by a tank division moving on to the front. In that barracks he found thirty kilograms of coffee. This was a virtual gold mine, as the German people would pay almost anything for coffee. They had not had real coffee since well before the war, and the German people loved good coffee. Jake traded the coffee for other supplies they needed. For example, on one occasion Jake traded a mere three hundred grams of coffee for seventy-two cigarettes, one hundred grams of tobacco, one pound of jam, one box of matches, one sausage, half a pound of macaroni, and ten eggs. Coffee was the currency that could buy them anything they wanted.

The Beautiful Temptation

While Jake's group was with the Americans, they continued their practice of going to the houses of local Germans and asking them to prepare a meal. They remained polite, and if someone declined, they would move on to the next house. As most Germans were still frightened and feeling somewhat guilty, very few refused their request.

Once free, Jake found his appetite to be insatiable. The group would eat several meals for breakfast, the same for lunch, and then again for dinner. They had nothing else to do during the day but eat. To this day, Jake still can't quite fathom how they ate as much as they did. Considering the portions they consumed, he would say it was impossible, yet they managed it.

One day they were out scouting for their fourth or fifth meal of the day when they saw a small castle in the distance. Jake thought it would make a good next stop, so off they went. They walked up to the front of the house and knocked on the door. The door opened and there was a young girl of about three years old with beautiful, blond, curly hair. She took one look at Jake and said, "Papi, Papi!" That was quickly followed by another voice from inside that pleaded, "Don't hurt my baby! Don't hurt my baby!" Jake responded that his group was different and that they had no intention of doing anything of the sort. With that, the person behind the voice came to the door.

The woman that appeared in the doorway was one of the most beautiful Jake had ever seen. She was a strikingly tall, blond German woman, about twenty-three years old. Jake repeated his usual request for a meal and promised she would come to no harm. Once he had finished, the woman unexpectedly burst into tears. She said she would be more than willing to cook them a meal, but that she didn't have any food to do so. While she had lots of money, that had become worthless after the war, and she wasn't able to buy any food. Also, her sister had tuberculosis, and she couldn't get proper food to help her get better.

After thinking for a few moments, Jake asked the girl if she could use some coffee to get the things she needed. Her face lit up. She responded that coffee was like gold, and that you could get anything you needed if you had coffee. So Jake gave her some of his coffee, enough to buy plenty of food for her and her sister. There was just something about that little girl mistaking him for her father that really moved Jake. The fact that he found the woman to be very beautiful didn't hurt either.

The lady's name was Elizabeth Slössher, and her sister was Veronica. They were living in that small castle together after Elizabeth's husband had been killed in the war. That's why her daughter mistook Jake to be her father; she was still waiting for him to come home. The little girl didn't yet understand that he was never going to do so. After that first visit, the sisters invited Jake and his group back several more times. Elizabeth always made sure they were well fed, and Jake made sure that she had everything she needed. Elizabeth's daughter would sit on Jake's knee for hours, imaging that he might indeed be her father.

Over the course of their visits, Elizabeth grew very fond of Jake. She began suggesting that he should stay there with her in Germany. While he liked her very much, he would always remind her that he had a girlfriend back home that we was very anxious to see again, and that Iet was the girl he was going to marry. Elizabeth persisted saying that in wartime things were different, and that people would understand. While Jake knew that might be true, he wouldn't have forgiven himself because he felt it would be wrong to forget Iet. But the offer was tempting. Elizabeth was a beautiful, intelligent, and funny woman, with a wonderful daughter and a very nice castle. Even when Jake was ready to leave, she begged him to stay. In the end, he said his farewells and began his long trek for home. As he could not take all the supplies that he had accumulated with him when he left, Jake gave the remainder (including the rest of the coffee) to Elizabeth, so that she could care for her family.

Jake never spoke to Elizabeth again, but he did receive a letter from her shortly after he returned home. It contained a large picture of Elizabeth and her daughter. In the letter she again told Jake that she really loved him and that she so badly wanted him to come back to her in Germany. Jake didn't reply to her appeal, as he was now happily back with his girlfriend. However, the letter ended up getting him in some trouble anyway. He left it lying around, and somehow Iet had managed to get her hands on it. She was very upset, as she felt it was proof that Jake had cheated on her while he was away, especially because he had not told her about Elizabeth. The picture only made matters worse, as Iet could see how beautiful Elizabeth was. After a lot of reassurance and explanation, Iet was finally convinced that Jake hadn't done anything wrong. But that letter almost cost Jake his relationship with his future wife.

While Jake never talked to Elizabeth again, he still speaks very fondly of her to this day. His eyes light up when he tells the story, especially when he talks about her beautiful little daughter. Jake doesn't regret for a moment that he went home, as his feelings for Iet were far stronger than those he had for Elizabeth. But had Iet not been in the picture, he just might have taken Elizabeth up on her offer.

Home Sweet Home

After staying five weeks with the Americans, Jake and his group finally received the news that they were going home. Not only that, but they were to travel home by plane, something none of them had ever done before. Jake could not have been more excited. The next morning, an army truck came to pick them up to take them to the airport, or so they supposed. Thirty-five men were loaded into a convoy of twelve trucks. Once everyone was onboard, the trucks drove off. Only they didn't head toward the airport. Instead they ended up taking Jake and his group back to the city of Erfurt, over one hundred kilometres in the wrong direction. This was a double blow to Jake. Not only was he not going home when he thought, but he was further away than before.

In Erfurt they were put to work guarding German prisoners, peeling potatoes, and running messages. It wasn't all bad, as they were well-fed and were given more shoes and clothing. But now they desperately wanted to go home.

Fortunately, their stay in Erfurt only lasted about five days. After that time was up, they were loaded into trucks and brought to the train station. While they wouldn't be flying home, at least now they were on their way. They traveled for three days and three nights on that train, criss-crossing much of Germany. The train eventually brought them to Munich, far in the south of Germany and, ironically, even further away from the town of Dirksland than they had been when they were in Erfurt.

Once they arrived in Munich, they were handed over by the Americans to the English. They were disinfected once again, and their papers were checked to ensure there were no German soldiers hiding in their midst. They were then fed and loaded on to trucks. This time they were definitely on their way back to the Netherlands. They traveled for miles through destroyed towns and villages, but by this time no one really noticed the carnage anymore. They were used to it by now, and their minds were full of thoughts of being home.

Jake crossed the border back into the Netherlands a full eleven months after he had first been sent from Kamp Amersfoort to Espenhain. The whole truck erupted into cheers and singing as the prisoners finally arrived back in their homeland. And then the truck promptly broke down. They had to sit by the side of the road waiting for the driver to get it fixed again. Fortunately, the problem was not too severe, and within ninety minutes they were on the road again.

The group's first stop in the Netherlands was in Enschede. As they pulled in, they were greeted by loud cheers from the locals and were given celebratory cigarettes. They stayed that night in an empty factory, and the next morning they were put through a full screening process. First there was a medical exam to ensure they were not carrying communicable diseases. Then they were interviewed by customs regarding any possible connections to the Nazis. Apparently, there were SS and Nazi collaborators who were trying to escape by pretending to be ex-prisoners. Out of the group of one thousand people that Jake was now traveling with, about twenty were arrested and taken away. The rest were now free to go where they pleased. Unfortunately, since there wasn't much public transit operating yet, they were advised to stay until transportation could be arranged. While he was waiting, Jake found a woman who was leaving for Rotterdam before him, and she offered to take a note to his family so the shock would not be too great for them when he got home. Until they received that note, they still had no idea whether he was alive or dead, as they had not heard from him in almost a year.

The next day Jake's group was brought to the town of Wezep, where they stayed for another day and a half. Next they went to Zwolle, where they were loaded on a boat to travel across the Ijselmeer to Amsterdam. When they arrived in Amsterdam, they were received to tremendous fanfare. There were throngs of people and bands playing music. They even got a mounted police escort from the boat to the train station. Once they made their way through the crowds, they boarded a train for Den Haag, where they were greeted to similar fanfare. Finally the train made its way to Rotterdam.

In Rotterdam there were more celebrations, but by this time Jake was entirely focused on seeing Iet. He went to her house in Rotterdam. His heart was in his throat at the thought of seeing his girlfriend again after such a long absence. When he knocked on the door, he was greeted by her parents. While they were very excited to see him, he quickly found out that, while Iet was well, she was staying in Dirksland at the moment. While disappointed, this setback only strengthened his resolve to get home as soon as possible.

After a good night's sleep in Iet's wonderfully soft bed, Jake boarded the train that would take him to Hellevoetsluis. From there he had to catch a boat to get to the island, and then he would finally be home. By this time he was getting extremely impatient, as it had been over two months since he had escaped from the camps. But he was to run into one more obstacle. When he got to Hellevoetsluis, he discovered that he would have to wait another five hours for the next ferry. He could see the water tower of his village across the channel, but he couldn't get there.

He started to look around to see if there were other boats going across. Just then an army jeep pulled up, and he saw two officers get out and head to a small military speed boat. Deciding he could wait no longer, Jake approached the officers and politely requested a ride across. At first they refused, as it was strictly forbidden to take civilians in that boat. But once Jake told them his story and they realized just how long he'd been trying to get home, they relented. They had him go below deck, where no one would see him, and they whisked him across to the island. They dropped him off just before they got into the harbor and wished him the best of luck.

When he came on shore, he was quickly spotted by his very good friend Leen Haack. Leen was very surprised to see him, as everyone had begun to think that he had died in Germany. The news he had sent ahead had not yet made it to the rest of the people on the island. Many other prisoners had already returned, but Jake had not been among them, so his friends began to assume the worst. But there he was in the flesh, and Leen couldn't have been happier. He quickly arranged for a motorcycle to bring Jake back to his home in Dirksland, which was still a few kilometres away.

Jake walked back into his house in Dirksland exactly 393 days after he was first arrested in Appeldorn. His mother and his two brothers were both there to greet him. Within minutes a motorcycle pulled up with Iet on the back, and the reunion was complete. Everyone's prayers had been answered. While Jake doesn't remember exactly what happened in that first day when he was back, he can still recall the wonderfully warm inner feeling he had at the notion of finally being home.

Chapter 7: Life after the War

Life returned to normal for Jake quite quickly after his return. While he spent the following day relaxing and talking with friends, the next day after that he returned to his work in the mill. There was much to be done, and soon it felt like he had never been away. While he would think about his experiences in Germany from time to time, they quickly faded into the background as the pressures of day-to-day life took over.

The Post-war Years in the Netherlands

The year after he returned, Jake married his girlfriend, Iet, and they settled down to start a family. Their first child, Arie, was born a year later in 1947, with their second, Peter, following in 1949. They would go on to have a total of five children, three boys and two girls (Arie, Peter, Nellie, Joanne, and Jacob Jr).

Jake worked hard in the milling business, and when he was twenty-three he had successfully paid off his remaining loans. As his mother was getting older, it was now time for him to formally take over the mill. Even though he had done much of the work to get the business on track and had made many of the improvements to the mill himself, he was obliged to buy the business from her at a top price. While economically it would have made more sense for him to start his own mill at half the cost, he decided that it was more important to support his mother at the inflated price. So he borrowed more money from an old miller friend and worked even harder to pay that loan off as well.

Jake was mostly happy in Dirksland after the war. He enjoyed married life and had a few very close friends he enjoyed spending time with. They were a supportive group that really looked out for each other. For instance, after the war Jake had bought a big, old army truck to use around the mill. While the truck used too much gas and constantly broke down, there weren't many other options at the time. A few years later, Opel introduced a small, more modern truck that was perfect for the mill. While Jake needed a new truck badly, he simply couldn't afford it—that was until the day his friend John loaned him the money he needed, interest free, with the understanding that Jake could pay it back whenever he was able.

Not everything in post-war Netherlands was quite so pleasant, however. The post-war government had become overly bureaucratic and too involved in people's lives. Jake remembers one incident in great detail. During the war, in order to feed the people they were hiding, Jake and Neil had acquired some animals, including a cow and some pigs. But after the war, the Dutch authorities came and said they were not licensed to keep such animals and gave them a five thousand-guilder fine. Given that a typical house would cost three thousand guilders, that was a huge amount. Jake was furious. He was being fined for keeping the very animals he had acquired to save people from the Nazis. Even worse, it was the wartime government of the Netherlands who, broadcasting over the BBC from London, had asked the Dutch people to help the resistance in this exact manner. He took the matter to court and explained his situation to the judge. The sympathetic judge replied that he was unable to change the law, even though he agreed with Jake. He simply did not have the power to overturn the violation. But what he did have the power to do was to change the amount of the fine, which he promptly lowered from five thousand guilders to fifty cents. Although gratified by this result, Jake was still very unimpressed with the whole system.

Jake and his family lived in Dirksland during the famous flood of 1953. A high spring tide, together with a large windstorm, had created a storm tide surge of over five metres. Some of the dikes around the low-lying islands were overwhelmed by the storm, and sea water had rushed in to flood many of the villages in the provinces of South Holland and Zealand.

Water ended up covering over thirteen hundred square kilometres of the Netherlands. All together, over twenty-four hundred people died in the flood, and thirty thousand animals drowned. There were also 47,300 buildings damaged, of which 10,000 were completely destroyed.[xxxvii] Some of the worst death and destruction occurred on Jake's home island of Goeree-Overflakkee. Fortunately for Jake and his family, the mill was built on a dike, and the house was high enough that it was not flooded. While they did not lose their lives or any of their own property during that event, they felt the economic repercussions nonetheless. Their customers' crops were destroyed in the flood, so for a year they had very little grain to mill. While others were insured for losses to their property and possessions, there was no insurance to cover Jake's business losses. Even so, he struggled through the hard times and returned the business to prosperity.

Emigrating to Canada

By the mid-1950s, Jake's brother Neil had decided to emigrate to Canada. He didn't like running his in-laws' family store in the Netherlands and wanted to have new adventures in Canada. He has always been more of a free spirit than Jake, so together with his wife, Mar, he just up and moved. Jake was settled in Dirksland and had no interest in leaving even though Neil was constantly pushing him to come over to Canada as well.

Jake might have stayed in the Netherlands his whole life if it weren't for a fire that destroyed the mill. While Jake had insurance to cover the cost of rebuilding the mill, the town had changed the building codes and wanted him to move the mill back on his property. Jake might have complied with this request, except that his insurance didn't cover the high cost of building a new foundation for the relocated building. So Jake was stuck. He finally gave the town an ultimatum; either they gave him permission to rebuild on his current site or he would take the insurance money and move to Canada. When the town didn't grant him the permission he needed by the date he specified, he made the decision to emigrate. Even though the town later came back with the approval he needed, Jake told them it was too late and that he had made his decision. On September 14, 1959, Jake and his family boarded the ocean liner the *Grote-Bear* and sailed across the Atlantic Ocean.

Upon arriving in Canada, Jake moved to the town of Lethbridge, in the Canadian prairie province of Alberta. He lived there happily with his family for a number of years. Sadly, in the early 1970s, his beloved wife, Iet, developed cancer. While she fought valiantly against the disease, she eventually lost the battle. She died on a Sunday morning, December 5, 1971. Iet had been the light of Jake's life, a wonderful mother to their children, and a well-liked member of the community. Without her, Jake felt lost and lonely. He went through a difficult time before he met and fell in love with another woman. Jake married his current wife, Elma, in 1973, and after an initial period of adjustment, has found new happiness in his second marriage.

Building Businesses

In his heart, Jake always had a passion for being in business for himself. He had been running the mill since he was a teenager, and that independent spirit came with him to Canada. Together with his brothers, he started a car dealership selling imported cars such as Volvos, Mercedes, BMWs, and DKWs. Even though they had their rocky times along the way, the business continued to grow, and they became the number one Mercedes dealer in the province of Alberta.

Unfortunately, to be successful in the car business, you had to be good at selling new cars and used cars. The challenge for Jake and his brothers was that, while they had no problem selling new cars, they struggled to compete in the used car business. Being successful in used cars required selling cars that are "less than perfect" to customers. If you took the time to ensure the car was in top shape, you would end up spending too much money and you would not be competitive. But Jake and his brothers just couldn't bring themselves to sell unsafe cars. So they always fixed them first or at minimum, told the potential buyer exactly what work needed to be done. Eventually they realized that their approach was going to continue to handicap them, so they decided to look for other opportunities.

The next business Jake and his brothers started was in the manufacturing sector. After finding a Dutch partner, Jake and his brothers opened Intercontinental Truck Body, a company that manufactures truck bodies, trailers, generator buildings, and other industrial use products. Together with his brothers, Jake helped grow ITB into a multi-million dollar business. He worked as manager until his retirement in 1993, when he and his brothers turned the reins of the business over to the next generation. His three sons Arie, Peter, and Jake Jr. all worked in the business over the subsequent decades. Arie retired from the company in 2006, while Peter and Jake still lead different divisions of the organization as general managers. The company that Jake and his brothers founded now employs over three hundred people in five operations in Canada and the United States.

The "Retirement" Years

Given his history, Jake wasn't the type of person to retire and play golf every day. As he backed away from his daily duties at ITB, he began to focus his efforts on growing his personal investments. He has become somewhat of an amateur investment guru over the years and has made a decent income from his portfolio. He still spends at least thirty minutes each day tracking his investments and planning for future stock purchases.

Jake is still happily married to his second wife Elma, and they remain very fit and active for people in their eighties. They both have the energy and vitality of people at least ten years younger. They walk every day and also ride their bikes around town. In addition, Jake goes swimming at the local pool with his younger brother Neil at least three times a week.

Jake has also had many adventures in his retirement years. He is an avid fan of recreational vehicles and still takes his motor home on trips in Canada and the United States. He also developed a love for sailing in his later years and, with his brother Hugo, purchased a thirty-five-foot sailboat. He moored the boat in the harbor in Point Roberts, Washington, and proceeded to sail around the coast of Washington state and British Columbia. He decided to build a cottage in Point Roberts so he could fully enjoy his stay there. While he has subsequently sold the boat, he still regularly visits his cabin in Point Roberts. And because he is younger in his mind than his actual years might suggest, he still drives the trip from his home in Coaldale, Alberta, to his cottage in Point Roberts in a single day, even though the journey covers more than twelve hundred kilometres.

While Jake and Elma have many of their own adventures, they always prioritize spending time with their children, grandchildren, and great-grandchildren. They visit most of their family on a regular basis and try to attend any of the important events that occur (baptisms, weddings, anniversaries, etc.) even if it means making a special trip to do so.

While this book focuses mainly on the period that Jacob Van Seters was imprisoned under the Nazi regime, his subsequent life has definitely been an amazing journey as well. He has run three different business, moved halfway around the world, raised a family, and lived long enough to see many grandchildren and great-grandchildren come into the world. He has endured the heartbreak of losing his beloved wife Iet and yet found new happiness in his current marriage to Elma. Throughout it all, he has remained close to God and is still unafraid of the challenges that life brings his way, knowing that God will provide him with the strength and courage to persevere.

Chapter 8: Thoughts for Future Generations

While Jake's story makes for a captivating but also a somewhat frightening tale, it is important to him that it is seen as more than just a story. By God's grace, most of us will not have to endure the type of suffering he did, so there are many lessons we can learn from someone who went through this type of ordeal. By no means does Jake claim to be a saint or even suggest that he did everything right. But he did survive in an environment where many others did not, and his hope is that others can learn something from his experiences so that some good comes from what was otherwise a very dark time in his life. The following are some of the key themes that he'd like to share with the future generations and more importantly, his future descendants.

Don't Behave Like an Animal

One of the decisions that Jake made very early on in his captivity was that he was going to try to continue to be a good, moral person, no matter what happened to him. He thought of the model that Jesus showed in the Bible when he did not allow himself to lash out at his captors, even though he had the ability to do so. Jake decided he would not allow the fact that other people treated him badly serve as an excuse for his own bad behavior. He felt that, just because people treated him like an animal (or worse), this did not give him the right to behave like one. In fact, he was convinced that if he could continue to hold the moral high ground as opposed to his captors, it would help him survive some of the mental hardships he was enduring and would keep him from giving up hope.

Maintaining a high moral standard was also a form of silent rebellion. The whole Nazi imprisonment system was structured to break people down, to degrade them and destroy their self-respect. The shaved head, the ill-fitting, lice-infested clothes, the forced marches, and the lack of cleaning facilities were all designed to break a person's spirit. If, through all that, a person could maintain some sense of dignity and retain a proper sense of right and wrong, then the Nazis had lost a major battle. This mindset was apparent in a number of the decisions that Jake made throughout his imprisonment.

Jake's first moral dilemma came as a result of the lack of food that the prisoners experienced. He felt that because the Germans had unfairly imprisoned him, and that they were not feeding him properly, that it was not wrong for him to steal food from them whenever he could. This explains why he had no problem relieving the Germans of some of their potato crop. But he did not extend this to include stealing from other prisoners, as many of those who were incarcerated chose to do. To Jake, his need to survive did not supersede that of his fellow prisoners. Also, as these people had done him no wrong and were in no way responsible for his treatment, he could not justify depriving them of whatever food they might have. On the other hand, Jake never considered himself above reproach, as he would still focus on his own survival first:

> I always had some people who leaned on me. I tried to help them and, if I had food, to divide it a little bit. Maybe I was selfish and took more for myself; I don't remember too well, but I suppose. I'm only human. I don't want to sound as if I was a saint; I wasn't a saint. I tried to be honest. Where I could help, I helped.

Jake also did not extend his self-given right to relieve the Germans of their possessions beyond taking the things he needed to survive. So while he was fine with stealing the roll of straw in Kamp Amersfoort, or the food coupons in Böhlen, he did not extend this activity to stealing money or possessions from the Germans. To Jake, the only things that he felt right in taking were the food and supplies that they should have given him in the first place. Even so, the decision to steal food still weighed heavily on him throughout his captivity.

A second area where Jake did not allow himself to lower his moral standards was in the treatment of the Germans following his escape. While he saw many other prisoners running rampant, killing, stealing, and raping the German population, Jake and his group chose to behave in a much more civilized manner. They did not feel that, just because they had been badly mistreated, they now had a moral right to behave in any way they chose. It was not their job to exact revenge, or to make the German people pay for what had happened to them. They still had to be the same courteous and respectful Christian people they had always been. While they may have been walking a fine moral line asking German families to prepare them meals, they did not stoop to threats or violence with any of these people. They simply asked for food, and if they were denied, they moved on to the next house. While they knew that the German people were afraid of what the prisoners would do to them, Jake's group always agreed that they would play no part in such mistreatment of civilians.

Jake also refused to act like an animal in another way. Even when his captors abused him, he would refuse to give up his rights on the most important things. Unlike a dog that slinks away after it has been beaten, Jake chose to stand up for himself when it really mattered. For instance, when he was being transported away from Kamp Amersfoort, he refused to sign the paper that stated he had received his possessions, when in fact he had not got them back. He did not let the Nazi guard intimidate him into giving up the ring, watch, and Bible that were so important to him. Also, when he was sick and needed to go to the sick bay, he did not just give in when the camp commander told him to return to work detail. He stood up for himself and insisted that he was unfit to work. However, he knew that he couldn't use this approach too often. If he had not chosen his fights carefully but had been defiant on every issue, he surely would not have lasted very long in the camps. For instance, if he had insisted on being allowed into the Germans-only bomb shelter during the March 21 air raid, there is little doubt that they would have taken him aside and put a bullet through his head. For any action, there is always an appropriate time and place.

Jake wasn't alone in trying to maintain a certain level of moral behavior as a defense mechanism against Nazi oppression. In her account of how she survived imprisonment in Auschwitz, *Surviving the Nazi Concentration Camps*, Bloeme Evers-Emden recalled the approach of the group of women she was with:

> Although they tried to drive home the idea of how worthless we were, just blode kuhe (stupid cows), we never felt we were unterenschen (sub-humans).... We helped each other as much as possible. We didn't use foul language, we upheld a high moral standard among ourselves and we consoled each other .... we succeeded, despite horrible conditions, in keeping a high moral standard. To a great extent that made it possible to prevent disintegration.[xxxviii]

Understand Your Adversary

Jake insists that one of the reasons he made it through his ordeal is that he understood the German system and the German people. This understanding of why they were doing certain things allowed him to make sense of the situation, even though he may not have agreed with what was going on. Without that understanding, it would have been easy to slip in to despair. When behaviors seem random and unpredictable, they are much harder to cope with. If he understood why things were happening, he felt much better equipped to deal with the results.

Understanding the system also helped Jake predict how the Germans would respond to his actions. He could predict when he would be able to push the limits, and when he would have to back off. As a result of the rigid structure of the German system, they were actually fairly predictable in their behavior and responses. Because he understood their system, Jake actually took back some control of his own destiny. While he could obviously not control everything, by being able to predict what the Germans would do, he could tailor his behavior to elicit the desired response. For example, when he pushed the guard at Kamp Amersfoort to return his personal possessions, he knew that the man needed to have his paperwork filled in correctly and that he did not have the authority to refuse once Jake had demanded to see the commandant.

Without the proper understanding of the enemy, Jake could have gotten himself killed many times over. For instance, when he was called in to explain how he had gotten the stolen potatoes, he knew that the German psyche would need some sort of answer. Being defiant and refusing to talk would likely have cost him his life. Instead he made up a plausible story, and because he was seen to be cooperating with the investigation, he was let go, even though the Germans did not find their "culprit."

Jake did not just rely on his past knowledge of the German system to survive; he became an active student while he was imprisoned. He was constantly talking to the Germans, asking questions, and observing their behavior. As the war progressed, he saw their behavior change, and he could then change his own tactics accordingly. Because he was constantly learning, he could adapt to his current situation. For instance, if he had tried to escape from the camp in February of 1945, he would have most certainly been caught and shot. But by April, the psyche and demeanor of his captors had changed to the point that he knew it was highly improbable that they would execute him for trying to escape.

Jake's knowledge of the German people also helped him greatly. For instance, once he had escaped, Jake knew that the Germans would be fearful of reprisals from the prisoners, and therefore they would likely fulfill any reasonable request that he and his group would make. He also understood that the bartender at the first bar where they stopped was unlikely to make a fuss when they didn't pay their bill.

Jake's approach to knowing your enemy applies to any situation of conflict in a person's life. Whether the enemy is an actual foreign army, whether it is prejudice and racism, or even if it is a deadly disease, the key to not letting that enemy be too overwhelming is to really understand it, to study it, and to become a student of it. Only then can a person retake as much control of his or her own destiny as possible in his or her given circumstance.

Bad Government Doesn't Mean Bad People

To this day, Jake holds little animosity to the German people for what happened to him. He believes that the Nazi party was evil and corrupt and that it attracted a small portion of the worst people in German society to it as co-conspirators. He does not apply this as a blanket condemnation of the German people. There were simply too many good Germans that were kind and helped him during his ordeal, even though they were under no compulsion to do so. There was the lady on the farm where Jake and John went to work, who not only gave them jobs but also gave them far more food than the situation required. She even gave them food to take back with them, a gesture they had never expected. Then there was the German farmer who allowed them to hide in his barn when they were caught in no-man's land between the German and American forces. And of course there were Elizabeth and Veronica Slössher, two German sisters who they became quite close to while they waited to go home.

While Jake wishes that the German people had stood up to their government much more than they did, he finds it hard to be too critical of them, considering what happened in his own country. While there has been much written about the Dutch resistance, in reality the number of people involved was a very small portion of the population. The rest either just stood by and did nothing or even worse, became co-conspirators. To Jake such behavior is unfathomable. It is easier for him to understand how the German people could have been complacent with their own government than how the Dutch people could have been so complacent with an invading force. The Dutch were so cooperative that, by the end of the war, a higher percentage of

Dutch Jews had died than in any other occupied country except for Poland, the country that contained the actual extermination camps.

Jake also saw immoral behavior from many different groups during his ordeal. This lack of morality was not the sole domain of the Nazis or their SS guards. Prisoners stole from other prisoners and would betray each other to the guards just to get some extra food. Recently freed prisoners went on killing and raping rampages, terrorizing the German people, many of whom had nothing to do with the SS or the Nazi party. And members of the Russian army behaved no better than animals as they stole, murdered, and raped their way across the German countryside. To Jake this in no way excuses anything that the Germans did, but for him it illustrates that things that happened in the war were not so black and white as some of the history books might suggest.

Just because Jake is at peace with the German people doesn't mean that he is at peace with the system that sent him away. In recent years, the German government introduced a reparation program to compensate those who had suffered under the slave labour programs. By the time this initiative had wrapped up in 2007, it had distributed 4.37 billion euros to 1.66 million people in over one hundred countries. But Jake refused to participate, as he felt that it was a half-hearted attempt to wipe the slate clean with the people who had been so abused. For Jake, there was no amount of money that could atone for what had happened to him.

Suffering Can Enrich the Rest of Your Life

While Jake would never wish his wartime experiences on another person, he does feel that the rest of his life has been richer because of what he went through. Specifically, he feels that he experiences the happiness in his life more intensely, that he is less tied to his personal possessions, and that he is more appreciative of the blessings he received from God.

First, because he has been to rock bottom, he feels that he can experience the high points in life with much more intensity. The range of emotion between where he was in the camps and where he is now is much larger than most people will ever get to experience. He compares it to the experience of sitting beside a warm fire. If you are inside and warm already, you only receive marginal pleasure from sitting next to a warm fire. But if you've been out in the cold, and then you come in and sit by that same fire, the feeling is many times more intense and enjoyable.

Second, because he had everything taken away from him once before, he has a true appreciation for the transient nature of possessions. As such, throughout his life, he has not been married to his possessions. While he enjoys the things he has, he has also been able to take risks in business that could have cost him everything he owned. Because he's been there once before, he truly realizes that everything can be taken away in a moment.

Finally, he appreciates the blessings he has today even more because of what he went through. He came so close to dying in the camps that he really sees everything he's received since as a bonus. He could have just as easily died in the camps as did so many others. But God had other plans for him and has blessed him richly with both a large family and with material success.

Leaders Step up When Needed

Jake didn't go into the camps looking to lead people. In fact, all he really wanted to do was get back home safely. Yet there were a number of times when he was called on to take a leadership role, and he took on the challenge when he was needed.

As discussed in chapter 2, Jake's first major experience in a leadership role occurred when his father died. There was no one left to lead the family, so Jake took it upon himself. Perhaps it was this early experience that prepared him for the number of times he would need to take a leadership role during his ordeal.

The first example of this occurred when he was stealing potatoes. He found the potato stash and then led two other prisoners to help steal the potatoes. And when it became too dangerous to continue, due to the fact that the pit could collapse, he advised those who were with him that it was time to stop. Those who didn't listen ended up getting caught and shot for their efforts.

Jake also played a lead role for his friend John when they decided to find work on one of the local farms. It was Jake who came up with the idea and then led John though the execution of the plan. As John was somewhat timid, he would have not been able to pull this off without Jake's leadership and drive.

Finally, Jake led the group of prisoners with whom he escaped. He not only convinced them to escape, but he also led them across the battlefield, led their interactions with the Americans, and helped them all choose the moral high ground when interacting with the German people. He was even chosen as the formal group leader during the time they spent with the Americans.

The key in all of these situations is that Jake did not go looking for leadership opportunities. He wasn't trying to be in control or wanting to tell others what to do. He just wanted to go home. And yet, when leadership was needed, he stepped up and delivered. He did not back down from the challenge to lead when it presented itself, and the people he led are much better off because of the choices he made.

Survival Takes Hope, Purpose, and Dedication

Surviving very difficult circumstances requires a combination of hope, purpose, and dedication. First, for Jake to survive, he needed to have some hope that he would eventually go back home. Even if that possibility was somewhat remote, he needed to be able to hold on to a future that was different than the present circumstances he was in. If he had lost that hope, he would have given up and died. But Jake always believed he was going to make it and that, in the end, he was going to go home. He simply did not believe he was going to die in that distant corner of Germany.

Second, this hope was coupled with a strong purpose. Jake needed to survive because there were many things he had to do back home. There was no one else to run the mill, and there were many improvements that still had to be made. Plus, his father had left him in charge of the family, and thus he had duties he needed to fulfill. He felt that God had a larger purpose for him and that God would see him through his suffering.

Jake spent a lot of time in the camps thinking about the mill. He thought about all the things that frustrated him and started planning how he was going to address them once he returned home. He hated mindless, needless manual labour, so he began thinking of ways that he would make the factory more efficient and automated. He also thought about how he would grow and expand the business into different areas. In his mind it became a foregone conclusion that he was returning home; it was no longer if but when. Not only did this daydreaming distract him from the hardships of his current reality, but it strengthened the sense of purpose he had for the future. Viktor Frankl talks about the importance of this "future focus" in his book *Man's Search for Meaning*:

> The prisoner who lost faith in the future—his future—was doomed. With his loss of belief in the future, he also lost his spiritual hold; he let himself decline and become subject to mental and physical decay.[xxxix]

Having this strong future purpose transformed his situation from wanting to survive to needing to survive. Because he felt he needed to survive, he was more willing to be dedicated to that goal and less willing to give up. Fulfilling a want can be a passing notion, easily given up in the face of hardship. Fulfilling a true need, on the other hand, comes from a much deeper place. If people feel they truly need to do something, they are much harder to dissuade than someone who merely wants to do it, no matter how intense that want may be.

Third, this hope and purpose needed to be supported by dedication. Jake needed to be absolutely disciplined and dedicated to the act of surviving if he was going to make it through his ordeal. He needed to ensure that he got enough food, even if that meant risking his life to steal if from the Germans. He needed to ensure he got enough sleep so that he would not die from exhaustion, even if it meant staying in bed during an air raid. He needed to ensure that he didn't eat spoiled or rotten food, no matter how hungry he was. He needed to ensure that he prayed constantly and read his Bible when he could. And he needed to ensure that he was wise in regard to his captors, that he did not let his emotions control his responses, but rather that he remained as in control of his actions and reactions as humanly possible. If he was missing any one of these factors, he believes he would have never made it back home.

"Fearing God, I Fear No One"

The most important message that Jake wants to leave to future generations and to anyone else who might read his story is that God is the one who carried him through his ordeal. When he thought he had no more strength to proceed, God gave him enough to make it through the day. And when God saw that Jake was at the limit of what he could bear, he ensured that nothing more was added to his plate.

For Jake, there is no other explanation. If he thinks about it logically, he should have died there in Germany. He was not so different from those who didn't make it. Yet he often received far less punishment and torture than they did. Plus he always seemed to be able to find a way to get a little more food, whether it was potatoes from the ground or fruit from the roadside.

In the end it was Jake's faith, his fear in God that allowed him to face his circumstances without being afraid. The following quote best sums up his feelings:

I said I had no fear, but that's not because I was so brave but because I fear the Lord and I know I was always in his hands.

He may have been depressed, upset, angry, and full of despair, but he was not afraid. That lack of fear enabled him to do things he would have never thought possible. In the end, that lack of fear kept him alive.

Appendix A: The Timeline of Jake's Ordeal

May 10, 1940—Germany invades the Netherlands

May 24, 1944—The planned date of Uncle Neil's wedding

May 23, 1944—Jake is arrested in Apeldoorn and taken to Kamp Vught

May 23–30, 1944—In cell in S'Hertogenbosch/Kamp Vught

May 30, 1944—Jake taken to Rotterdam by Dutch couriers

June 1–July 7, 1944—Jake in jail in "Het Haagsche Veer"

July 7, 1944—Jake transferred to concentration camp in Amersfoort

July 7–July 20, 1944—Jake at concentration camp in Amersfoort

July 20, 1944—Jake transferred from Amersfoort to Espenhein

December 1944—Jake transferred to Böhlen

February 19/20, 1945—Bombing of Böhlen, Operation Thunderclap

March 20, 1945—Bombing of Böhlen, factory destroyed

Early April, 1945—Jake escapes camp at Böhlen

April 18, 1945—Jake goes back to Böhlen to get last possessions

April 18, 1945—250 slave labourers killed by SS in Leipzig massacre

April 19, 1945—American tanks roll into Böhlen and officially take over

April 18–May 2, 1945—Jake's group bikes toward the Netherlands

May 2–June 10, 1945—Jake has to wait after bikes are confiscated

June 10, 1945—Jake taken back to Erfurt

June 15–18, 1945—Jake travels across Germany by train for three days

June 18, 1945—Jake arrives in Munich and takes a truck to the Netherlands

June 18—21, 1945—Jake circles the Netherlands by train

June 21, 1945—Jake returns home, thirteen months after being arrested

January 27, 1946—Jake writes his first account of his time in the camps

Appendix B: Maps of Jake's Journey

The Journey to Germany[xl]

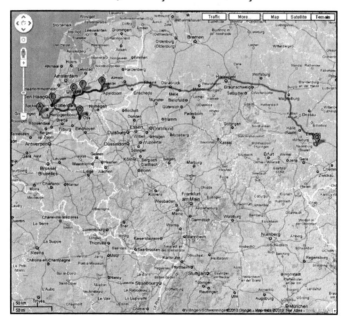

A. Dirksland, the Netherlands

B. Apeldoorn, the Netherlands

C. Utrecht, the Netherlands

D. S'Hertogenbosch, the Netherlands

E. Rotterdam, the Netherlands

F. Amersfoort, the Netherlands

G. Espenhain/Bohlen, Germany

The Journey Home^{xli}

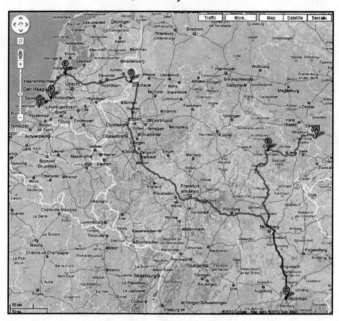

A. Espenhain/Bohlen, Germany

B. Erfurt, Germany

C. Munich, Germany

D. Enschede, the Netherlands

E. Amsterdam, the Netherlands

F. Rotterdam, the Netherlands

G. Dirksland, the Netherlands

References

i. *Book of Praise*, Anglo-Genevan Psalter, Premier Printing, Winnipeg, Maintoba, Canada, 1998, 133.

ii. Anthony Andersen, "A Forgotten Chapter: Holland under the Third Reich," http://www-lib.usc.edu/~anthonya/waralt.htm.

iii. Ibid.

iv. Ibid.

v. Michael Englishman, *163256: A Memoir of Resistance*, Wilfred Laurier University Press, Waterloo, Ontario, Canada, 2007, 5.

vi. Anthony Andersen, "A Forgotten Chapter: Holland under the Third Reich," http://www-lib.usc.edu/~anthonya/waralt.htm

vii. Wibke Bruhns, *My Father's Country*, Bond Street Books, Toronto, Ontario, Canada, 2008.

viii. http://en.wikipedia.org/wiki/Kamp_Vught

ix. http://www.tijm.nl/rubriek2a/holocaust/stadswandeling_rotterdam.htm

x. Primo Levi, *Survival in Auschwitz; If This Is a Man*, BN Publishing, Thousand Oaks, California, 2007, 16.

xi. http://en.wikipedia.org/wiki/Kamp_Amersfoort

xii. http://en.wikipedia.org/wiki/Westerbork

xiii. http://en.wikipedia.org/wiki/Nazi_concentration_camps

xiv. http://en.wikipedia.org/wiki/Extermination_camps

xv. http://en.wikipedia.org/wiki/Arbeitslager

xvi. http://www.personal.ceu.hu/students/06/Nationalism_Media/mobWWII.ppt.

xvii.   http://documentatiegroep40-45.nl/dwangarbeid_oud/camps.htm

xviii. http://www.geschichtskultur-ruhr.de/archiv/essen001103/fasse.pdf

xix.   http://en.wikipedia.org/wiki/Extermination_through_labor

xx.   Benjamin Ferencz, *Less than Slaves*, Indiana University Press, Bloomington, Indiana, 2002.

xxi.   http://de.wikipedia.org/wiki/BRABAG

xxii.   http://www.airpower.maxwell.af.mil/airchronicles/aureview/1981/jul-aug/becker.htm

xxiii. http://de.wikipedia.org/wiki/Arbeitserziehungslager

xxiv.   Ibid.

xxv.   http://de.wikipedia.org/wiki/BRABAG

xxvi.   Viktor Frankl, *Man's Search for Meaning*, Beacon Press, Boston, Massachusetts, 2006, 30.

xxvii. Primo Levi, *Survival in Auschwitz; If This Is a Man*, BN Publishing, 2007, 66.

xxviii. Viktor Frankl, *Man's Search for Meaning*, Boston, Massachusetts, Beacon Press, 2006, 5.

xxix.   Primo Levi, *Survival in Auschwitz; If This Is a Man*, BN Publishing, Thousand Oaks, California, 2007, 21.

xxx.   http://www.merwedegijzelaars.nl/?page=foto&id=37

xxxi.   http://en.wikipedia.org/wiki/Bombing_of_Dresden_in_World_War_II

xxxii. Viktor Frankl, *Man's Search for Meaning*, Beacon Press, Boston, Massachusetts, 2006, 31.

xxxiii. Joel Berman, *Slave Labor; A Meditation on Humanity*, Juniper Springs Press, Apple Valley, California, 2007, 57.

xxxiv. Elie Wiesel, *Night*, Hill and Wang, New York, New York, 2006, viii–ix.

xxxv.   Joel Berman, *Slave Labor; A Meditation on Humanity*, Juniper Springs Press, Apple Valley, California, 2007.

xxxvi. http://commons.wikimedia.org/wiki/File:Buchenwald_Zeitz_Mass_Grave_80916.jpg

xxxvii. http://en.wikipedia.org/wiki/North_Sea_flood_of_1953

xxxviii. Bloeme Evers-Emden, "Surviving the Nazi Concentration Camps," http://www.aasd.k12.wi.us/VOS/Textbook_Links/SS/7th/docs/175.pdf

xxxix. Viktor Frankl, *Man's Search for Meaning*, Beacon Press, Boston, Massachusetts, 2006, 74.

xl. Map from Google Maps (maps.google.com), copyright 2010 Google Map Data, copyright 2010 Tele Atlas.

xli. Map from Google Maps (maps.google.com), copyright 2010 Google Map Data, copyright 2010 Tele Atlas.

LaVergne, TN USA
02 July 2010
188228LV00002B/40/P